Bhakti-rasāyana

BOOKS BY
ŚRĪ ŚRĪMAD BHAKTIVEDĀNTA NĀRĀYAṆA GOSVĀMĪ MAHĀRĀJA

Arcana-dīpikā
Beyond Nīrvāṇa
Śrī Bhajana-rahasya
Śrī Bhakti-rasāmṛta-sindhu-bindu
Bhakti-tattva-viveka
Śrī Brahma-saṁhitā
Essence of the Bhagavad-gītā
Five Essential Essays
Going Beyond Vaikuṇṭha
Harmony
Jaiva-dharma
Letters From America
Śrī Manaḥ-śikṣā
My Śikṣā-guru and Priya-bandhu
Pinnacle of Devotion
Śrī Prabandhāvalī
Secret Truths of the Bhagavatam
Secrets of the Undiscovered Self
Śiva-tattva
Śrī Bṛhad-bhāgavatāmṛta
Śrī Camatkāra-candrikā
Śrī Dāmodarāṣṭakam
Śrī Gauḍīya Gīti-guccha
Śrī Gītā-govinda
Śrī Gopi-gīta
Śrī Harināma Mahā-mantra
Śrī Navadvīpa-dhāma-māhātmya
Śrī Navadvīpa-dhāma Parikramā
Śrī Prema-sampuṭa
Śrī Rādhā-kṛṣṇa-gaṇoddeśa-dīpikā
Śrī Saṅkalpa-kalpadrumaḥ
Śrī Śikṣāṣṭaka
Śrī Upadeśāmṛta
Śrī Vraja-maṇḍala Parikramā
Śrī Rāya Rāmānanda Saṁvāda
Śrīla Bhakti Prajñāna Keśava Gosvāmī – His Life and Teachings
The Distinctive Contribution of Śrīla Rūpa Gosvāmī
The Essence of All Advice
The Gift of Śrī Caitanya Mahāprabhu
The Journey of the Soul
The Nectar of Govinda-līlā
The Origin of Ratha-yātrā
The Way of Love
Utkalikā-vallarī
Vaiṣṇava-siddhānta-mālā
Veṇu-gīta
Walking with a Saint
Rays of the Harmonist (periodical)

For further information, free downloads of all titles,
world tour lectures, and more, please visit our websites:

www.purebhakti.com
www.purebhakti.tv
www.backtobhakti.com
www.bhaktistore.com

śrī śrī guru-gaurāṅgau jayataḥ

Bhakti-rasāyana

Śrī Śrīmad
Bhaktivedānta Nārāyaṇa
Gosvāmī Mahārāja

VṚNDĀVANA • NEW DELHI • SAN FRANCISCO

Bhakti-rasāyana, 4th edition, 2nd printing

First edition:	November 1994 – 1,000 copies
Second edition:	November 1997 – 2,000 copies
Third edition:	September 2006 – 1,000 copies
Fourth edition:	September 2011 – 2,000 copies
	May 2013 – 2,000 copies

Printed at Spectrum Printing Press Pvt. Ltd.,
New Delhi (India)

ISBN 978-1-935428-37-4

Library of Congress Control Number 2011937004

British Library Cataloguing in Publication Data. A catalogue record for this book is available from the British Library

Cataloging in Publication Data--DK
Courtesy: D.K. Agencies (P) Ltd. <docinfo@dkagencies.com>

Bhaktivedānta Nārāyaṇa, 1921-
Bhakti-rasāyana / Bhaktivedānta Nārāyaṇa Gosvāmī Mahārāja. -- 4th ed.
p. cm.
Includes verses in Sanskrit (roman); with English translation.
Includes index.
ISBN 9781935428374

1. Bhakti in literature. 2. Krishna (Hindu deity) in literature. 3. Vaishnava poetry Sanskrit--History and criticism. I. Title.

DDC 294.5925 23

Contents

Publisher's Note

The Path of Love

The soul's nature is to seek real freedom, to hanker for lasting pleasure. We seek satisfaction and happiness in the world around us, but our experiences over time expose the futility of such ephemeral pleasure. Enlightened souls, who are full of compassion, describe the reality of a permanent bliss based on a lasting spiritual existence. Their writings provide us with an intimate insight into reality, which is replete with variety, form, qualities and exquisite, lustrous personalities. Their writings also invite us to participate in the sweetness of ever-increasing transcendental love, or *prema*. They thus direct us to that ultimate destination, which is achieved by attaining the spiritual perfection that they themselves possess. What they describe is called the path of love, distinct among the philosophies of India as *bhakti-yoga*, or devotion to God.

The Great Master

Bhakti-yoga is the essence of the Vedas (India's vast body of ancient Sanskrit scriptures; *veda* means "knowledge"). It is the path that all paths ultimately lead to, since it reveals the topmost condition of the heart. Although *bhakti-yoga* has been practised since time immemorial, the *bhakti-yoga* movement underwent a renaissance five hundred years ago in Bengal, coinciding with Europe's own Renaissance period.

The leading figure and reformer of this *bhakti* movement was Śrī Kṛṣṇa Caitanya, also known as Mahāprabhu, 'the Great Master'. The general populace of India regard Śrī Caitanya Mahāprabhu as a most extraordinary saint, but actually, He is an *avatāra*, an incarnation of the Lord who comes to this world with a specific mission.

He chose to incarnate as compassion personified in order to benefit the world in the troubled Age of Kali (our current epoch, the age of quarrel and hypocrisy).

According to Śrī Caitanya Mahāprabhu, worldly social distinctions are utterly irrelevant to one's eternal spiritual identity, which can easily be realized by chanting the names of God in the *mahā-mantra* – Hare Kṛṣṇa, Hare Kṛṣṇa, Kṛṣṇa Kṛṣṇa, Hare Hare, Hare Rāma, Hare Rāma, Rāma Rāma, Hare Hare.

The Mahā-mantra

The Hare Kṛṣṇa *mahā-mantra* is Śrī Rādhā and Śrī Kṛṣṇa personified as sacred sound. The vibration of the *mantra* is not a material sound as it comes directly from the spiritual platform and is beyond the realm of the mind. One can chant it all day and night and never feel tired. The more one chants, the more our spiritual consciousness is revived. The *mahā-mantra* consists of three words: Hare, Kṛṣṇa, and Rāma. Each word is in the vocative, a calling out to Rādhā and Kṛṣṇa.

Kṛṣṇa is the source of all spiritual potency and Śrī Rādhā is the complete embodiment of that potency. She is known as Hara (one who steals away) because She can captivate Kṛṣṇa's mind. In the vocative case, "Hara" becomes "Hare". Because He bestows bliss upon the residents of Vṛndāvana, He is referred to as Kṛṣṇa, the all-attractive one. The extraordinary beauty of His transcendental form always surcharges the minds and senses of the cowherd damsels and the other residents of Vraja with ever increasing spiritual bliss. For this reason He is glorified as Rāma.

The Supreme Form of Godhead

Śrī Kṛṣṇa (God) has many forms. All of them are perfect, but the Vedic scriptures state that Śrī Kṛṣṇa's original form in Vṛndāvana is the 'most perfect'. That holy abode is fully resplendent with His sweetness, which even predominates over His divine opulence. The residents of that holy place are imbued with such elevated feelings for the Supreme Lord that their worship of Him is devoid of the reverence normally offered to God. Those with a parental relationship with Him chastise Him, His friends defeat Him in games and order Him about, and His beloved *gopīs* sometimes become angry with Him and refuse to speak with Him. Such familiar and charming exchanges please Him unlimitedly more than exalted, reverential prayers offered by persons who do not have the same purity of love for Him.

In his preface to *Kṛṣṇa, The Supreme Personality of Godhead,* Śrīla Bhaktivedānta Svāmī Mahārāja states, "Kṛṣṇa is all-attractive, one should know that all his desires should be focused on Kṛṣṇa. In the *Bhagavad-gītā* it is said that the individual person is the proprietor or master of his own body but that Kṛṣṇa, who is the Supersoul present in everyone's heart, is the supreme proprietor and supreme master of each and every individual body. As such, if we concentrate our loving propensities upon Kṛṣṇa only, then immediately universal love, unity and tranquillity will be automatically realized. When one waters the root of a tree, he automatically waters the branches, twigs, leaves and flowers; when one supplies food to the stomach through the mouth, he satisfies all the various parts of the body."

This book, which reveals wonderful truths about the Supreme Person, will satisfy any sincere seeker of the Truth.

About the Author

On the auspicious day of Maunī Amāvasyā, 1921, Śrī Śrīmad Bhaktivedānta Nārāyaṇa Gosvāmī Mahārāja took his divine birth in a devout Vaiṣṇava family in Tivārīpura, in the state of Bihar, India.

In February, 1946, he met his *gurudeva,* Śrī Śrīmad Bhakti Prajñāna Keśava Gosvāmī Mahārāja, and his life of complete and exemplary dedication to Gauḍīya Vaiṣṇavism, or the path of *kṛṣṇa-bhakti* in the line of Śrī Caitanya Mahāprabhu, began.

He accompanied his *gurudeva* on his extensive preaching tours throughout India, actively assisting him in propagating the teachings of Śrī Caitanya Mahāprabhu for the eternal benefit of the living entities in this world. This included regularly hosting the thousands of pilgrims attending the yearly circumambulation of Śrī Navadvīpa-dhāma, the appearance place of Śrī Caitanya Mahāprabhu and Śrī Vṛndāvana-dhāma, the appearance place of Śrī Kṛṣṇa.

His *gurudeva* had instructed him to translate the writings of prominent Gauḍīya Vaiṣṇavas into Hindi, a task he assiduously assumed throughout his entire life and which resulted in the publication of nearly fifty Hindi sacred texts. These invaluable masterpieces are currently being translated into English and other major languages of the world.

For many years, he travelled throughout India to spread the message of Gauḍīya Vaiṣṇavism, and it was for this end, also, that in 1996, he journeyed abroad. During the next fourteen years, he circled the globe more than thirty times. Whether he was in India or abroad, his preaching always bore the distinctive characteristic of boldly unmasking any misconception obscuring the specific purposes of Śrī Caitanya Mahāprabhu's advent, in strict adherence to the desire of Śrīla Bhaktisiddhānta Sarasvatī Ṭhākura Prabhupāda and in perfect congruence with the conceptions of Śrīla Rūpa Gosvāmī, Śrī Caitanya Mahāprabhu's foremost follower. Thus, in present times, in upholding the glorious tenets of the Gauḍīya *sampradāya*, he performed the function of a true *ācārya*.

❊❊❊❊❊

At the age of ninety years, on December 29, 2010, at Cakra-tīrtha in Śrī Jagannātha Purī-dhāma, he concluded his pastimes in this world. The following day, in Śrī Navadvīpa-dhāma, Śrī Gaurasundara's fully empowered emissary, the very embodiment of His unique compassion, was given *samādhi*. He will never cease to reside in his divine instructions and in the hearts of those who are devoted to him.

nitya-līlā-praviṣṭa oṁ viṣṇupāda
Śrī Śrīmad Bhaktivedānta Nārāyaṇa Gosvāmī Mahārāja

nitya-līlā-praviṣṭa oṁ viṣṇupāda

Śrī Śrīmad Bhaktivedānta Vāmana Gosvāmī Mahārāja

nitya-līlā-praviṣṭa oṁ viṣṇupāda
ŚRĪ ŚRĪMAD BHAKTIVEDĀNTA SVĀMĪ MAHĀRĀJA

nitya-līlā-praviṣṭa oṁ viṣṇupāda
ŚRĪ ŚRĪMAD BHAKTI PRAJÑĀNA KEŚAVA GOSVĀMĪ MAHĀRĀJA

nitya-līlā-praviṣṭa oṁ viṣṇupāda
ŚRĪ ŚRĪMAD BHAKTISIDDHĀNTA SARASVATĪ PRABHUPĀDA

Here the *gopīs* are mutually hearing and describing Kṛṣṇa pastimes, and as remembrance comes, they are seeing Kṛṣṇa with the eyes of *bhāva*. It appears that they are suffering due to separation, but inside them is great happiness. (Page 52)

During the day while playing and jumping about with His *sakhās*, if Kṛṣṇa, desiring to see the splendour of the forest, would go to a somewhat distant place, then with great speed the *sakhās* would run to Him saying, "I will touch Him first! I will touch Him first!" and in this way they enjoyed life. (Page 89)

For the purpose of increasing their eagerness, sometimes Kṛṣṇa hides, and then the *sakhās* are unable to stay where they are and they begin searching for Him. If one of them catches a glimpse of Him, then at once they all race there. One after the other, they embrace Kṛṣṇa, and laughing, Kṛṣṇa embraces them in return. (Page 92)

"Neither Brahmā, Śiva, nor even Lakṣmī-devī – who eternally resides at Kṛṣṇa's chest in the form of a golden line – has ever received as much mercy as Yaśodā did from He who is the bestower of liberation." (Page 147)

"Those *vraja-gopīs* who had fully given their hearts to Śrī Kṛṣṇa, would imitate His manner of speaking and His activities. Since they had offered their very souls to Him and always sang His glories, they completely forgot themselves and their family interests." (Page 159)

But upon seeing Kṛṣṇa, one will have no desire to remove one's gaze from Him because He always appears new and fresh. One will perpetually remain thirsty to drink the nectar of His appearance and will never desire to look away. (Page 166)

Introduction

At the beginning of the second part of Śrīla Sanātana Gosvāmī's *Śrī Bṛhad-bhāgavatāmṛta*, Jaimini Ṛṣi explains to Janamejaya how, after having heard the description of Nārada's quest that comprises the first part of this exalted scripture, Parīkṣit Mahārāja's mother Uttarā said to her son, "My heart cannot be satisfied if those devotees who, being indifferent to any other spiritual practice and spiritual attainment, desire only the eternal service of Śrīmatī Rādhikā, and who perpetually sing Her glories and are immersed in love for Her, attain residence in merely the same Vaikuṇṭha as so many other devotees do. This is a matter of great sorrow! And I cannot tolerate that this may be the final destination for devotees like Śrī Nandarāya and Śrī Yaśodā. There must certainly be a suitable abode for them that is superior to Vaikuṇṭha. If there is such a place, then please describe it and deliver me from this doubt." (*Bṛhad-bhāgavatāmṛta* (2.1.21–2, 24))

Parīkṣit Mahārāja replied, "Although I could satisfy you by answering your question with the words of the Śruti and Smṛti, instead, by the mercy of my spiritual master, Śrī Śukadeva, I will first relate a historical narration that will dispel all of your doubts. Then I will speak those essential verses of the scriptures." (*Bṛhad-bhāgavatāmṛta* (2.1.34–5))

Then, after hearing the incomparable story of Gopa-kumāra that comprises the second part of the *Bṛhad-bhāgavatāmṛta*, Janamejaya said to Jaimini Ṛṣi, "Fearing that these descriptions will now come to an end, my heart is feeling great sorrow.

Therefore now please give me such potent nectar that, upon hearing which, my heart will be fully purified for all time." (*Bṛhad-bhāgavatāmṛta* (2.7.89))

Jaimini replied, "O my child Janamejaya, your father, Śrī Parīkṣit, feeling transcendental pleasure upon describing the glories of Goloka, next sang with a wonderful and sweet devotional mood numerous verses from two great epics that are the very essence of the Śrutis and Smṛtis. With great happiness I wander in this world singing these verses, thereby mitigating the pangs of separation from your father that I feel." (*Bṛhad-bhāgavatāmṛta* (2.7.90–1))

Then Jaimini Ṛṣi went on to quote four verses from *Brahma-saṁhitā* and fifty-nine verses from *Śrīmad-Bhāgavatam* that collectively have come to be known as *bhakti-rasāyana*, nectar-tonic that stimulates devotion unto the Supreme Lord Śrī Kṛṣṇa. This book is a translation of lectures spoken originally in Hindi by our esteemed Śrīla Gurudeva, *oṁ viṣṇupāda aṣṭottara-śata* Śrī Śrīmad Bhaktivedānta Nārāyaṇa Mahārāja. Spoken in 1991 at Śrī Keśavajī Gauḍīya Maṭha in Mathurā, this material comprises his commentary on twenty-eight of these verses that are the very essence of the Tenth Canto of *Śrīmad-Bhāgavatam*. In gradation these verses glorify the devotion of the different classes of devotees in Vraja, culminating in the topmost *bhakti* of the *vraja-gopīs*.

In his ongoing publication of Vaiṣṇava literature in the English language, Śrīla Gurudeva mentions repeatedly that he is simply following in the footsteps of his dear friend and instructing spiritual master, *nitya-līlā-praviṣṭa oṁ viṣṇupāda* Śrī Śrīmad A.C. Bhaktivedānta Swami Prabhupāda. Śrīla Prabhupāda single-handedly and in a relatively short period of time spread the teachings of Kṛṣṇa consciousness around the entire world. His translations and writings set the standard for the literary presentation of Vaiṣṇava philosophy, and we sincerely pray that our current efforts are pleasing to him.

Grateful acknowledgement is extended to Lavaṅga-latā dāsī for copy-editing this new third edition, to Śānti dāsī for proofreading the final manuscript, to Atula-kṛṣṇa dāsa for checking the Sanskrit, to Kṛṣṇa-prema dāsa for designing the new cover and to Subala-sakhā dāsa for providing the new photograph of Śrīla Gurudeva. It is the earnest prayer of all of us serving in Gauḍīya Vedānta Publications that Śrīla Gurudeva, who is the very embodiment of a *rasika* Vaiṣṇava, be pleased with our efforts. We offer obeisances to him time and again for giving us such wonderful explanations of the nectar-tonic that Parīkṣit Mahārāja gave to Uttarā, Jaimini Ṛṣi gave to Janamejaya, and Sanātana Gosvāmī gave to the inhabitants of this world.

An aspiring servant of the Vaiṣṇavas,

Prema-vilāsa dāsa

the holy day of Śaradīya-pūrṇimā
10th October, 2003
Gopīnātha-bhavana, Śrī Vṛndāvana

Maṅgalācaraṇa

oṁ ajñāna-timirāndhasya
jñānāñjana-śalākayā
cakṣur unmīlitaṁ yena
tasmai śri-gurave namaḥ

I offer my most humble prostrated obeisances unto the spiritual master, who has opened my eyes, which were blinded by the darkness of ignorance, with the torchlight of knowledge.

vāñchā-kalpa-tarubhyaś ca
kṛpā-sindhubhya eva ca
patitānāṁ pāvenebhyo
vaiṣṇavebhyo namo namaḥ

I offer obeisances to the Vaiṣṇavas, who just like desire trees can fulfil the desires of everyone and who are full of compassion for conditioned souls.

namo mahā-vadānyāya
kṛṣṇa-prema-pradāya te
kṛṣṇāya kṛṣṇa-caitanya-
nāmne gaura-tviṣe namaḥ

I offer obeisances to Śrī Caitanya Mahāprabhu, who is Kṛṣṇa Himself. He has assumed the golden hue of Śrīmatī Rādhikā and is munificently distributing *kṛṣṇa-prema*.

he kṛṣṇa karuṇā-sindho
dīna-bandho jagat-pate
gopeśa gopikā-kānta
rādhā-kānta namo 'stu te

I offer obeisances to Śrī Kṛṣṇa, who is an ocean of mercy, the friend of the distressed and the source of all creation. He is the master of the *gopas* and the lover of the *gopīs* headed by Śrīmatī Rādhikā.

tapta-kāñcana-gaurāṅgi
rādhe vṛndāvaneśvari
vṛṣabhānu-sute devi
praṇamāmi hari-priye

I offer obeisances to Śrīmatī Rādhikā, whose complexion is like molten gold and who is the queen of Vṛndāvana. She is the daughter of Vṛṣabhānu Mahārāja and is very dear to Śrī Kṛṣṇa.

hā devi kāku-bhara-gadgadayādya vācā
yāce nipatya bhuvi daṇḍavad udbhaṭārtiḥ
asya prasādam abudhasya janasya kṛtvā
gāndharvike nija gaṇe gaṇanāṁ vidhehi

O Devī Gāndharvikā, in utter desperation I throw myself on the ground like a stick and with a choked voice humbly implore You to please be merciful to this fool and count me as one of Your own.

aṅga-śyāmalima-cchaṭābhir abhito mandīkṛtendīvaraṁ
jāḍyaṁ jāguḍa-rociṣāṁ vidadhataṁ paṭṭāmbarasya śriyā
vṛndāraṇya-nivāsinaṁ hṛdi lasad-dāmābhir āmodaraṁ
rādhā-skandha-niveśitojjvala-bhujaṁ dhyāyema dāmodaram

Whose dark bodily lustre is millions of times more beautiful than the blue lotus flower, whose refulgent yellow garments rebuke the radiance of golden *kuṅkuma*, whose residence is Śrī Vṛndāvana-dhāma, whose chest is beautified by a swinging *vaijayantī* garland, and whose splendorous left hand rests upon the right shoulder of Śrīmatī Rādhikā – I meditate upon that Śrī Dāmodara.

bhaktyā vihīnā aparādha-lakṣyaiḥ
kṣiptāś ca kāmādi-taraṅga-madhye
kṛpā-mayi tvāṁ śaraṇaṁ prapannā
vṛnde numaste caraṇāravindam

Devoid of devotion and guilty of committing unlimited offences, I am being tossed about in the ocean of material existence by the turbulent waves of lust, anger, greed and so forth. Therefore, O merciful Vṛndā-devī, I take shelter of you and offer obeisances unto your lotus feet.

gurave gauracandrāya
rādhikāyai tad-ālaye
kṛṣṇāya kṛṣṇa-bhaktāya
tad-bhaktāya namo namaḥ

I offer obeisances to the spiritual master, to Śrī Gauracandra, to Śrīmatī Rādhikā and Her associates, to Śrī Kṛṣṇa and His devotees, and to all Vaiṣṇavas.

vairāgya-yug-bhakti-rasaṁ prayatnair
apāyayan mām anabhīpsum andham
kṛpāmbhudhir yaḥ para-duḥkha-duḥkhī
sanātanaṁ taṁ prabhum āśrayāmi

I was unwilling to drink the nectar of *bhakti* possessed of renunciation, but Śrī Sanātana Gosvāmī, being an ocean of mercy who cannot tolerate the sufferings of others, made me drink it. Therefore I take shelter of him as my master.

śrī-caitanya-mano-'bhīṣṭaṁ
sthāpitaṁ yena bhūtale
svayaṁ rūpaḥ kadā mahyaṁ
dadāti sva-padāntikam

When will Śrī Rūpa Gosvāmī, who has established the mission in this world that fulfils the internal desire of Śrī Caitanya Mahāprabhu, give me shelter at his lotus feet?

yaṁ pravrajantam anupetam apeta-kṛtyaṁ
dvaipāyano viraha-kātara ājuhāva
putreti tan-mayatayā taravo 'bhinedus
taṁ sarva-bhūta-hṛdayaṁ munim ānato 'smi

I offer obeisances to Śrī Śukadeva Gosvāmī, who can enter the hearts of all living entities. When he left home without undergoing the purificatory processes such as accepting the sacred thread, his father Vyāsa cried out, "Oh my son!" As if they were absorbed in that same feeling of separation, only the trees echoed in response to his call.

tavaivāsmi tavaivāsmi
na jīvāmi tvayā vinā
iti vijñāya devi tvaṁ
naya māṁ caraṇāntikam

I am Yours! I am Yours! I cannot live without You! O Devī (Rādhā), please understand this and bring me to Your feet.

Bhakti-rasāyana

Chapter One

The Earth Becomes Fortunate

In the final chapter of *Śrī Bṛhad-bhāgavatāmṛta*, after the story of Gopa-kumāra has been completed, Sanātana Gosvāmī quotes verses from the Tenth Canto of *Śrīmad-Bhāgavatam* that Parīkṣit Mahārāja spoke to his mother, Uttarā. They are verses of very beautiful poetry that stimulate the sentiment of *bhakti*. Stringing these verses together, Sanātana Gosvāmī has composed a necklace for the benefit of the *sādhakas* of this world, and when *sādhakas* keep these verses in their hearts, it is as if they are wearing this necklace around their necks. And if while chanting the holy name they sometimes call out these verses, it will increase the spiritual pleasure (*ānanda*) in their chanting. This compilation of verses is known as *bhakti-rasāyana*, the nectar-tonic of devotional mellows. When the material body becomes weakened by illness and one is unable to eat anything, by drinking tonic the digestion and the pulse again become strong. Similarly, in the realm of *bhakti*, for those in whom intense hankering for spontaneous devotion (*rāgānuga-bhakti*) has arisen, the verses in this final chapter are like nectar-tonic. In the mood of Kamala Mañjarī, his eternal identity within Kṛṣṇa's pastimes, Bhaktivinoda Ṭhākura prayed:

nāhaṁ vande tava caraṇayor dvandvam advanda-hetoḥ
kūmbhīpākaṁ gurum api hare nārakaṁ nāpanetum
ramyā-rāmā-mṛdutanulatā nandane nābhirastuṁ
bhāve bhāve hṛdaya-bhavane bhāvayeyaṁ bhavantam

"O Lord, I am not performing *bhajana* so that You will remove the worldly misery that is strangling me. I am not praying at Your feet for entrance into the heavenly garden of Nandana-kānana where one can enjoy with beautiful women for a very long time, nor am I praying for liberation so that I will never again have to suffer for nine months in the womb of a mother and never again be punished by the messengers of Yamarāja. I pray that in the core of my heart You will increase the *bhāva* of Vṛndāvana, where You are roaming with the *gopīs* and enjoying amorous pastimes. In meditation on the descriptions of these pastimes, I will at once become completely lost in *prema* – *this* is what I am praying for. I am praying that I may take birth as a *gopa* or *gopī*, or even as a peacock or tree or anything, anywhere within the sixty-four square-mile Vraja-maṇḍala. There I will acquire the company of a *rasika* devotee who, being full of the *bhāva* of Vṛndāvana, will describe all of these pastimes to me, and then my life will be meaningful."

When *sādhakas* study and learn these verses, deeply meditating within themselves on their meanings while chanting the holy name, they will act as stimuli to fully experience the mood described in the verse above. Then one's mind will not wander here and there. We should not just walk around talking to others while chanting, but taking our chanting beads we should sit in a solitary place and give it our mind and heart. Our previous *ācāryas* chanted all night long, meditating on one verse after another. For half an hour the waves of the *bhāva* of one particular verse would be coming to them: sometimes they would be fully submerged in those waves, sometimes they would rise to the surface and float on those waves, and then they would move on to the next verse. As they did this more and more the whole night would pass, and where it went, they wouldn't know. *This* is the traditional method of performing *bhajana*.

Through these verses Parīkṣit Mahārāja is making the *bhakti* of his mother steady and strengthening her determination for *gopī-bhāva*, and through these same verses Sanātana Gosvāmī is nurturing us. There is a blend of so many different *bhāvas* in Vṛndāvana, but in the end, applying some polish to these sentiments, he emphasises *gopī-bhāva*. There are many verses here, and they are all beneficial to the cultivation of *bhajana*. To develop and strengthen this *bhāva* within us, we will study these verses in sequence, and from this endeavour intense hankering for this particular devotional sentiment will certainly arise within us.

dhanyeyam adya dharaṇī tṛṇa-vīrudhas tvat-
pāda-spṛśo druma-latāḥ karajābhimṛṣṭāḥ
nadyo 'drayaḥ khaga-mṛgāḥ sadayāvalokair
gopyo 'ntareṇa bhujayor api yat-spṛhā śrīḥ

Śrīmad-Bhāgavatam (10.15.8); *Bṛhad-bhāgavatāmṛta* (2.7.107)

[Śrī Kṛṣṇa said to Balarāma:] Today this land, along with all its green grass, has become fortunate due to receiving the touch of your lotus feet. And receiving the touch of the fingers of your lotus hands, the trees, creepers and bushes consider that they have attained the greatest treasure. Receiving your affectionate glances, the rivers, mountains, birds and animals are all feeling fully gratified. But most fortunate of all are the *vraja-gopīs*, who have been embraced to Your strong chest, a favour that even Lakṣmī-devī herself always desires.

This verse describes the time when Kṛṣṇa is at the junction of His *paugaṇḍa-līlā* (ages six to ten) and *kaiśora-līlā* (ages ten to sixteen). At this time His full beauty and charm are becoming more apparent, and His limbs are filling out. He would feel shy if He were to remain naked at this age. Now He enjoys taking the cows out to graze, and jumping about and creating mischief with His friends. At this age His form is like a bud that is beginning to open; it has not yet become a flower, but it is gradually opening and becoming more charming. Previously no fragrance came from the bud, and no bee would have been hovering around it. But as it opens more and more, the fragrance begins to come and there is nectar available to the bee. When it spreads out and becomes fully mature, it means that Kṛṣṇa has reached the *kaiśora* age. Now that Kṛṣṇa and Baladeva have become a little older, their forms have become very charming. Their feet have also become bigger; previously they were thin from heel to toe, but now like ripe bananas their feet have become big and very soft, and whereas before the soles of their feet had yellowish complexions, now they have begun to take on a reddish hue. Now Kṛṣṇa has become a little clever in speaking; instead of always speaking directly, He has learned to speak in a roundabout way. These are all symptoms of this age.

His newfound cleverness in speech is evident in His speaking of this verse. To avoid praising Himself, He uses the presence of Baladeva Prabhu as a pretext to express His feelings. Because at this age He has "become" a little intelligent, He realises that He should never praise Himself; praising oneself is like committing suicide. Here He wants to describe how Vṛndāvana is more glorious than any place within the three worlds, and even more glorious than Vaikuṇṭha. He begins by saying that the Earth is fortunate. Why is the Earth fortunate? Because of the presence of India. Why is India so glorious? Because of the presence of Vṛndāvana. And why is Vṛndāvana so glorious? Because of the presence of the *gopas* and *gopīs*. Why are the *gopas* and *gopīs* glorious? Because amongst them are Kṛṣṇa and Rādhā. And why are They glorious? Because of the mutual *prema* between Them, and that is our highest objective. If not for the amorous love of Śrī Rādhā and Kṛṣṇa, then all of our endeavours would be meaningless. It is prayed for again and again by the topmost devotees, and Rādhā's *prema* is so glorious that it overpowers Kṛṣṇa Himself.

But He doesn't describe all of this directly by saying, "I am the supreme ornament that beautifies Vṛndāvana." Because He is now entering His *kaiśora* age, when speaking He knows how to keep this feeling hidden and how to skilfully reveal it.

Together Kṛṣṇa and Balarāma are taking the cows out to graze, and upon seeing the beauty and splendour of the Vṛndāvana forest, at once Kṛṣṇa becomes overwhelmed with emotion. What is the meaning of "Vṛndāvana"? It means the forest of *vṛndā*, or *tulasī*. There are many other wonderful trees and plants found there, but the *tulasī* tree is primary. It can also mean the forest where the cowherd girl Vṛndā-devī is queen. Why is she known as the queen of Vṛndāvana? Because she arranges amorous meetings between Śrī Rādhā and Kṛṣṇa. Another meaning of *vṛndā* is "group", meaning groups of cows, *gopas* and *gopīs*, and *avana* can mean "one who nourishes and protects". So Vṛndāvana can also mean the ones who provide stimuli that nurture and increase feelings of love in Śrī Govinda and the cows, *gopas* and *gopīs*. More meanings have been given, but these three are primary.

As Kṛṣṇa was speaking this verse, He was remembering His own pastimes, and waves of *bhāva* began to flow inside Him. As He was going along with His friends, the joy He felt knew no limits, and He said, "My dear brother, today Pṛthivī-devī (the Earth) has become fortunate, and the hairs of her body, which are the grass, creepers, vines and trees, are standing on end in ecstatic rapture. The grass, creepers and vines, receiving the touch of your lotus feet, and the trees, being touched by your hands as you pick fruits and flowers, have today become fully gratified. And the rivers, mountains, birds, deer and all other animals, receiving affectionate glances from you, have today become especially fortunate. But the most fortunate of all are the *gopīs*, who have received what even Lakṣmī-devī herself desires – being embraced between your two strong arms."

From the very beginning of creation, Pṛthivī-devī has been serving Bhagavān. Whenever he desired to assume an incarnation, he would descend on this Earth and grace the land with his footprints. Varāha held the Earth on his snout, and at that time Pṛthivī-devī became his wife, and from them a son, Narakāsura, was born. And the Earth is always in contact with the Lord's form of Śeṣa as he holds her on his head. From time immemorial she has been receiving such good opportunities, but Kṛṣṇa tells Balarāma, "Today, by receiving the touch of your feet, the Earth has become especially fortunate. Why? Because you are now at the junction of your *paugaṇḍa* and *kaiśora* ages and your lotus feet are especially soft, and such a nice fragrance is coming from them. You move along the Earth like an intoxicated baby elephant. Has the Earth ever received such an opportunity before? Today the Earth has really become fortunate."

Here someone may point out that at that time Kṛṣṇa had been in contact with the Vṛndāvana forest for only ten-and-a-half years, whereas Śrī Rāmacandra wandered in the forest of Dandakaranya for fourteen years. In bare feet he also walked the entire distance to South India before entering Lanka, so did Pṛthivī-devī not become as fortunate then as she did during *kṛṣṇa-līlā*? But Rāma was banished to the forest, and when in the last year of his exile Rāvaṇa kidnapped Sītā, he wandered here and there crying in anguish. Therefore at that time Pṛthivī-devī certainly became fortunate from the touch of his feet, but she must have also felt very sad. She really became fortunate when Kṛṣṇa came in an immensely beautiful form; with a peacock feather in His crown, He would smile as He was decorated by His mother in the morning, and then, accompanied by Śrīdāmā and Subala and the other *sakhās*, He would take the cows out to graze and jump about with the calves. Just as the young offspring of a deer playfully jump about, He would go along with all of His friends with a happy heart. Picking flowers with their own hands, they would make garlands and decorate each other, and arriving at places like Kusuma-sarovara, Rādhā-kuṇḍa and Śyāma-kuṇḍa, they would enjoy pastimes that were saturated with *rasa*. With special care Kṛṣṇa would string one garland that was not meant for any of the *sakhās*, and feeling great happiness as He thought of whom He would place this garland on, He tucked it away. Who can estimate the great good fortune of those flowers, being picked and made into a garland by Kṛṣṇa's own beautiful hands? When in the evening He would place that garland on a certain devotee, He would feel supremely blissful. Did any of this happen in *rāma-līlā*? There was constant heartbreak in Rāmacandra's pastimes, but in contrast in *kṛṣṇa-līlā* there was so much carefree happiness.

In the same way as we may caress one person whom we love and lovingly slap another, Bhagavān has touched the Earth in different ways in his different incarnations. Rāmacandra touched the Earth, and Nṛsiṁhadeva also touched the Earth. Assuming a fearful form, Nṛsiṁhadeva appeared, and being extremely angry he killed Hiraṇyakaśipu. All of the residents of the heavenly and lower planetary systems were petrified with fear, and at that time the Earth did not experience great pleasure. But when Kṛṣṇa touched the Earth in such a beautiful form, she really became fortunate.

The rivers, especially the Yamunā, also became fortunate. At that time Mānasī-gaṅgā was also a river, though now it is in the form of a pond, and it also became fortunate. He would lovingly glance towards the rivers because there He would sport with the *gopīs* and *sakhās*. The rivers would make a sweet sound as they flowed gently, and bees would be hovering around the blooming lotuses. The soft breeze would carry the fragrance, and the entire scene would be so beautiful. Through the bestowal of His affectionate glances, He would also shower the nectar of His kindness upon the hills and mountains, because near them were very attractive *kuñjas* where there would be very beautiful grass, and on the pretext of taking the cows to graze He would go there. Sitting on the large rocks with His friends, they would decorate one another. These *kuñjas*, such as the ones near Kusuma-sarovara, were very beautiful, and there He would enjoy with the *gopīs* as well.

This verse describes four benedictions: receiving Kṛṣṇa's affectionate glances, receiving the touch of His feet, receiving the touch of His hands and being embraced by His arms, as the *gopīs* were. When Kṛṣṇa would be taking the cows out to graze, from hidden positions the *gopīs* would lovingly glance at Him, and then He would glance towards them with such affection that it would immerse them in remembrance of His sweetness. In the same way He would glance towards the different birds and animals, and from this they also became fortunate. Sometimes a peacock, being maddened in *bhāva*, would come near Him, and He would gently stroke it with His hand. Sometimes He would call a parrot, and when it flew onto His hand, while stroking it gently He would teach it to speak and then listen to what the parrot said back. The calves would also receive the touch of His hands. Very young calves – perhaps only a few days old – forgetting the company of their mothers, would jump along as they accompanied Kṛṣṇa to the forest. As they proceeded further and further, they would become fatigued, so Kṛṣṇa would take them on His lap and massage their legs, and with great love He would speak sweet words to them. Tell me – how much good fortune did those calves possess? He would also take the *sakhās* on His lap and stroke them, and in this way Subala and others received the touch of His hands. Considering the diverse sentiments of the residents of Vṛndāvana, He touches them in different ways. When Kṛṣṇa takes the cows and His friends to drink from and sport in the rivers, the rivers have one type of sentiment, and when He goes there with the *gopīs*, they have a different type of *bhāva*. Receiving the touch of Kṛṣṇa's feet, the rivers swell in spiritual ecstasy. The trees have the sentiment of *sakhās*, and they receive the touch of both His hands and feet. The cows have the sentiment of being His mother, and the calves have the sentiment of *sakhās*. The creepers have the devotional feelings of *sakhīs*, and when He picks flowers from them, it is as if He is teasing a *gopī* with His touch. The *gopīs* also receive the touch of Kṛṣṇa's lotus feet:

yat te sujāta-caraṇāmburuhaṁ staneṣu
bhītāḥ śanaiḥ priya dadhīmahi karkaśeṣu
tenāṭavīm aṭasi tad vyathate na kiṁ svit
kūrpādibhir bhramati dhīr bhavad-āyuṣāṁ naḥ

Śrīmad-Bhāgavatam (10.31.19)

[The *gopīs* said:] O dear one, Your lotus feet are so soft that we place them gently on our breasts, fearing that they will be harmed. Our life rests only in You, and therefore our minds are filled with anxiety that Your tender feet might be wounded by pebbles as You roam about on the forest path.

The *gopīs* are arguing with their own minds. Their minds are saying to them, "Why are you worrying about Kṛṣṇa? There is no necessity."

But from deep within their hearts, from their very souls, the *gopīs* reply, "We are upset because Kṛṣṇa's feet are very soft, and we are afraid that they will be pricked by thorns and pebbles. We desire that He should never feel any pain."

"Is Kṛṣṇa blind? He has eyes, doesn't He? He can see where to place His feet while walking."

"O mind, the calves run here and there, and do they only go to safe and smooth places? They run near the mountains, rivers and jungles, and they also have hooves that protect them from sharp objects. But if Kṛṣṇa goes to such places, His feet will be burned by the hot sand or pricked by thorns and pebbles. O mind, you have no intelligence!"

"But in Vṛndāvana there are no such thorns and pebbles. Everything here is *viśuddha-sattva*. They appear to be ordinary thorns, but it is as if they are made of rubber. Will rubber thorns prick your feet? They give a very soft touch to Kṛṣṇa's tender feet when He steps on them. And the pebbles are softer than butter! By the influence of *viśuddha-sattva*, Pṛthivī-devī has decorated her landscape with these soft and golden pebbles so Kṛṣṇa will never feel any pain."

In this way they were arguing with their minds. The *gopīs* received the touch of those feet in the *rāsa* dance, a benediction that even Lakṣmī-devī desires, and Brahmā is also always meditating on those feet:

āhuś ca te nalina-nābha padāravindaṁ
yogeśvarair hṛdi vicintyam agādha-bodhaiḥ

Śrīmad-Bhāgavatam (10.82.48)

Such great storehouses of knowledge as Lord Brahmā, Lord Śiva, the Kumāras and Śukadeva Gosvāmī are always trying to remember Kṛṣṇa's lotus feet, but only with great difficulty do those feet appear in their meditation. Responding to Kṛṣṇa's teasing with jealous anger, the *gopīs* say, "You have instructed us to meditate, but realisation of You rarely comes even in the meditation of the most highly learned devotees! We want You to come back to Vṛndāvana. And those feet that are being meditated on by so many – we desire to play with them directly. What to speak of holding them within our brains in meditation, we desire to hold them close to us. Meditation will not satisfy us, so we won't do it!"

They desire to receive the touch of His feet while they are decorating Him, and then they will also receive the touch of His hands. And in the end they will receive the benediction of being embraced between His two strong arms. Kṛṣṇa will be touching their feet also, when they exhibit jealous anger (*māna*) and He is trying to appease them. Then everything is reversed, and Lakṣmī also desires all of this.

So in this verse, when Kṛṣṇa says, "My dear brother, today the Earth has become glorious," He is simply using the presence of Baladeva Prabhu as a pretext so that the sweetness of Kṛṣṇa Himself, the sweetness of the *gopīs*, and the glories of Vṛndāvana can all be specifically described. And why has Vṛndāvana become glorious? Because in that place the grass and creepers received the touch of Kṛṣṇa's feet, its vines and trees received the touch of His hands, and its rivers, mountains, birds and animals received His affectionate glances. But above all Vṛndāvana is especially glorious because of the presence of the *gopīs*, whom Kṛṣṇa Himself serves.

Chapter Two

The Peacocks Dance to Kṛṣṇa's Flute Melody

After preparing lunch for Kṛṣṇacandra and Baladeva, Yaśodā along with Nanda Bābā follows them for a great distance as they take the cows out to graze for the day. Finally, after bidding them farewell for the day, they return home. After cooking for Kṛṣṇa, Śrīmatī Rādhikā and Her *sakhīs* return to Yāvaṭa. As Rādhikā's *sakhīs* sit near Her, each of them in their own specific parties as *taṭastha* (neutral), *svapakṣa* (belonging to Rādhikā's own group) and *suhṛt* (friendly), they all begin to meditate on Kṛṣṇa. They become deeply spellbound, and when He sometimes appears to their internal vision, they become enthralled in the mellow of divine separation (*viraha-rasa*). Seeing how Rādhikā is especially immersed in *viraha-rasa* and oblivious to all external considerations, the *sakhīs* call out to Her and bring even more remembrance of Kṛṣṇa's pastimes to Her by speaking this verse:

vṛndāvanaṁ sakhi bhuvo vitanoti kīrtiṁ
yad devakī-suta-padāmbuja-labdha-lakṣmi
govinda-veṇum anu matta-mayūra-nṛtyam
prekṣyādri-sānv-avaratānya-samasta-sattvam

Śrīmad-Bhāgavatam (10.21.10); *Bṛhad-bhāgavatāmṛta* (2.7.108)

O *sakhī* Rādhā, Vṛndāvana is more glorious than the heavenly planets, Vaikuṇṭha, and even more glorious than Ayodhyā and Dvārakā-purī, because it has been graced with the footprints of the son of Devakī. And only in this Vṛndāvana are the peacocks dancing in rhythm to the flute melody of Govinda. Hearing the sound of the flute and seeing the peacocks dancing, all of the birds, animals and other living entities have become stunned.

Here "Devakī" refers to the other name of Yaśodā, so in this verse *devakī-suta* means Yaśodā-nandana Kṛṣṇa, and His footprints are beautifying Vṛndāvana. When Akrūra and later Uddhava went to Nandagrāma, they saw these footprints everywhere. Seeing them, Akrūra fell down to offer obeisances and rolled on the ground, and crying profusely said, "Today I am so fortunate to have the *darśana* of Kṛṣṇa's lotus feet!"

Playing very deep notes on the flute, Govinda enters the forest near Govardhana. Immediately all the peacocks approach Him making the *ke-kā* sound, and they see that He appears like a dark raincloud. Because He uses the end holes of the flute to produce very deep notes, His playing of the flute is like thunder, and His yellow cloth is like lightning. The peacocks become maddened, and forming a circle around Kṛṣṇa, they begin dancing with great *bhāva* to the flute melody. Hearing the sound of the flute, all *sattva* – meaning "living entities" – become stunned and abandon their usual course of activities; animals such as tigers and bears even abandon their violent natures. *Sattva* can also mean that everything in the spiritual world is *viśuddha-sattva*, comprised of pure spiritual energy. There is not a touch of mundane qualities of goodness (*sattva*), passion (*rajas*) or ignorance (*tamas*) in that realm. There are so many objects in Vaikuṇṭha, and they are all *viśuddha-sattva*. Especially it is known as the essence of the *hlādinī* and *saṁvit* potencies combined, which is found in the hearts of the eternal *rāgātmikā* devotees there. If greed arises in the heart of a living entity for the sentiment of those devotees and he performs *bhajana* following in their footsteps, then when even one molecule of their devotion reflects into his heart, it can be called *sattva*. There are three kinds of *sattva*: *viśuddha-sattva*, *sattva* and *miśra-sattva* [*miśra* means "mixed"]. *Miśra-sattva* exists within the conditioned souls, *sattva* within the liberated souls who have not yet developed *bhakti*, and *viśuddha-sattva* within the *dhāma* and Bhagavān's eternal associates.

Here, with some jealous anger, the *gopīs* are revealing the feelings of their hearts: "All of the animals, birds, insects and everything of Vṛndāvana has become fortunate. In an independent way Kṛṣṇa is bestowing His touch on everyone and everything in Vṛndāvana. When He climbs the hills His feet are placed here and there, and even the trees and flowers are receiving His touch. But there is no possibility of us receiving this benediction, and therefore in Vṛndāvana we are the most unfortunate people."

As we mentioned before, there are thorns in Vṛndāvana also, but before Kṛṣṇa steps on them they become softer than butter. Experiencing the touch of His feet, they melt in divine bliss. With jealous anger the *gopīs* are saying, "As of yet our hearts have not become similarly melted in *kṛṣṇa-prema*; therefore if we could become thorns or blades of grass in Vṛndāvana, our lives would then become successful. For us there are so many obstacles. We are not able to go before Him and touch His feet and speak with Him. We are not able to fan Him or serve Him in any way during the daytime; there are so many restrictions upon us, but there are no such restrictions whatsoever for all of the other living entities in Vṛndāvana. If we were to become blades of grass, or thorns, or vines, or ponds, or the dust of Vṛndāvana, we could receive His touch; but in this form it is not possible." Here, in expressing their jealous anger, they are describing the good fortune of the land of Vṛndāvana. They go on to say that Bhagavān is also present in heaven in the form of Vāmana, in a form with thousands of heads and in other forms also. Although he is also present in these forms, they are partial forms; all incarnations are not equal. Those incarnations that possess more of the Lord's qualities, potencies and *rasa* are superior. Kṛṣṇa, Rāma and Nṛsiṁha possess more of these in comparison to other incarnations, and are therefore known as *parāvastha-avatāras*. But of these three, Kṛṣṇa is *avatārī*, the source of all incarnations, and the very basis of all *rasa* – *raso vai saḥ*. So because He is sporting there, Vṛndāvana is the most glorious place.

In his commentary on this verse, Sanātana Gosvāmī says that Kṛṣṇa played *mṛdu-mandra* on the flute. What is the meaning of *mṛdu-mandra*? When rainclouds begin to gather, the sky at once becomes dark, and very softly and slowly thunder comes. When the clouds clash violently it produces loud thunder and lightning also, but at first they produce a very soft and deep thunder, and that is called *mandra*. Kṛṣṇa produced a similar sound on the flute, but with *mṛdu*, sweetness. The nature of the peacock is such that when it sees the sky darkening and hears thunder, it begins dancing madly. When Kṛṣṇa entered the forest, what did He see? Girirāja-Govardhana resplendent with creepers, blooming flowers and ripe fruits. The breeze was blowing very gently, seemingly unable to carry the full weight of the flowers' fragrance. Seeing this natural splendour, the desire for enjoyment arose in Kṛṣṇa, and He played the flute very softly. Hearing this deep vibration, the peacocks went mad, dancing in rhythm with their tail-feathers fully spread out. Then all of the animals, birds and insects of Vṛndāvana congregated in the meadows of Govardhana to witness the performance.

The peacocks thought, "He is playing such a beautiful melody, and dancing to that we are feeling great joy, but we have nothing to offer Him in return."

After professional actors enact some of Bhagavān's pastimes, they place a deity of Kṛṣṇa or Rāmacandra on a plate and approach the audience for contributions. Seeing that others have placed some money on the plate, everyone feels obliged to give something. There is some intimidation or psychology used in this method. But when someone wants to give of their own free will because they genuinely appreciated a performance, they will reach in their pocket and no matter what note they first pull out – whether it is two rupees, five rupees or ten rupees – they will give it immediately. So one of these peacocks was thinking, "I have nothing valuable to offer Him – no golden necklace around my neck or any valuable ornaments. I am simply an animal, but the feathers of my tail are very valuable! There is nothing in this world that can compare to their beauty, and upon seeing them everyone becomes pleased. With their seven colours they are so attractive, so is there any reason why I shouldn't offer Him one?" Therefore he left behind one of his feathers.

Seeing it Kṛṣṇa thought, "This peacock is very loving; he has fully appreciated My flute-playing, and offered Me one of his valuable feathers. There is nothing artificial in this offering." Lifting the feather up and placing it on His head, He thought, "Just as the flute is dear to Me, this peacock feather has now become dear to Me. While walking, resting, dreaming, standing or sitting, I will never abandon it. Wherever I may go in Vraja, I will never abandon the flute or this peacock feather." This is the origin of the peacock feather becoming Kṛṣṇa's most celebrated ornament.

The peacock saw, "Oh, I left that feather for Him, but He didn't merely put it in His pocket! He has placed it on His head, the most valuable of all His bodily parts! Today my life has become completely successful."

If we desire to offer a gift to our spiritual master, to a Vaiṣṇava or to Bhagavān, but upon receiving it they were to say, "What need do I have for this? I have millions of good quality things," we would feel pain in our hearts. But instead they accept it and say, "Oh, what a beautiful thing you have brought me!" and then we feel very pleased. Similarly Sudāmā Vipra brought Kṛṣṇa some uncooked low-grade rice, and honouring his offering, Kṛṣṇa snatched it from him saying, "Oh, such a nice snack you have brought Me!" And even though it was uncooked, dry and tasteless, He immediately chewed it up and said, "Rukmiṇī and Satyabhāmā have never offered Me anything this nice!" Hearing this, how did Sudāmā Vipra feel? "Today I have become fully gratified."

So the peacock saw that he had offered Kṛṣṇa such a trivial gift, yet Kṛṣṇa had taken it and placed it on His head. Then Kṛṣṇa played the flute with so much *prema* that He became maddened along with the peacocks. The words *anu matta* in this verse generally refer to the peacocks becoming intoxicated, but it can refer to Kṛṣṇa as well. Then He played the flute with even more *prema*, and the peacocks became more maddened, Kṛṣṇa also became more maddened, and in this way there was competition between them. If someone offers something with *prema*, and it is also accepted with *prema*, then both parties become the tasters of that *prema*, and that is precisely what happened here.

While Kṛṣṇa was playing the flute in this way and the dancing was going on, all of the *sattva*, meaning the birds and animals, became motionless and watched and listened. But don't consider them to be like the birds and animals of this world; the birds and animals of Goloka are all *viśuddha-sattva*, and there is no trace of *tamas*, *rajas* or material *sattva* in them. Even when the living entity becomes very elevated, perhaps just before liberation, still there is some trace of material *sattva* in him. But in this world most people are *tamasika*, which means they are affected by lower attributes such as hatred, envy, anger and the cheating propensity. Then there is *rajasa*, which is characterised by intense greed for enjoyment. So even when *sattva* comes, at first it will be mixed with *tamas* and *rajas*. In the case of Hariścandra Mahārāja,[1] he gave away a great amount in charity, which is *sattvika*, but it was mixed with *rajas*. Karṇa was very charitable, always spoke the truth and did good to others, which are all *sattvika* qualities, but he was affected by anger, envy and the tendency towards violence, so it was mixed with *tamas*. Bharata Mahārāja[2] showed affection for an animal, which was *sattvika*, but still it was not *śuddha-sattva*. Only after the *jīva* attains *svarūpa-siddhi* and will imminently enter into *vastu-siddhi* can it be said that he is in *viśuddha-sattva*. Bhagavān and all of His devotees in Vaikuṇṭha, whether they are peacocks or monkeys or whatever, are situated in *viśuddha-sattva*.

In order to watch Kṛṣṇa playing the flute and see the dancing of the peacocks, many other birds gathered in groups on the branches of the trees of Govardhana. Below in the forest the deer were also watching, but with their eyes closed, as if in meditation. How could they be watching if their eyes were closed? By *sañcārī,* which means that they were internally experiencing the particular *sthāyibhāva,* permanent devotional sentiment, that they were situated in. There were a great many species of birds and animals watching from the meadows of Govardhana, and they all displayed the natures of sages. *Govinda-veṇum anu matta-mayūra-nṛtyam* – the name Govinda comes from the words *go* and *indate*. *Go* means the *gopas*, *gopīs*, cows and calves. It can also mean Veda, *brāhmaṇa*, knowledge, the senses and many other things. *Indate* means *indra*, which means master. So Govinda means "the one who increases the esctatic joy of everyone in Vraja by the notes He plays on the flute". Hearing this divine sound, all living

1. The story of Hariścandra Mahārāja is narrated in *Śrīmad-Bhāgavatam*, Ninth Canto, Chapter 7.

2. The story of Bhārata Mahārāja is narrated in *Śrīmad-Bhāgavatam*, Fifth Canto, Chapters 7–8.

entities forget their normal course of activities. At this time of the day, the birds generally make different sounds in their chirping such as *che-cha* and *kala-rava*, but all of these activities stop, and everyone forgets even their own bodies. This is the meaning of *avaratānya*. In this way everyone stands motionless, just listening and watching, thinking, "Aho! This can only be found in Śrī Vṛndāvana! Bhagavān is also present in Vaikuṇṭha, but there the sound of the flute cannot be heard. In Ayodhyā and Dvārakā one won't see peacocks dancing like this. This can only be found in Vṛndāvana, and nowhere else." *Vitanoti* means that Vṛndāvana is more glorious than the heavenly planets or even Vaikuṇṭha. There Kṛṣṇa exhibits four special qualities: *rūpa-mādhurī* (His extraordinary beauty), *veṇu-mādhurī* (the sweet, mellow sound of His flute), *līlā-mādhurī* (His supremely captivating pastimes) and *prema-mādhurī* (the especially sweet love that His companions in Vraja have for Him). Because Govinda is playing the flute there, the splendour and glories of Vṛndāvana are being proclaimed as the best of all.

How did Kṛṣṇa appear to the peacocks as He was playing the flute? He had the peacock feather placed in His crown, and He was standing in His threefold-bending posture with His right foot wrapped around His left. Seeing this, at once the joy of the peacocks increased. Kṛṣṇa was adorned with a garland of *guñja* flowers, which also included *kadamba* flowers and *tulasī* buds, that hung down to His knees. A mild fragrance was coming from it and bees were swarming around it. He was wearing bracelets on His wrists, and on His limbs were paintings of spiders. In this way Nanda-nandana was decorated in His forest attire, and He was holding the flute, which has been called His dear *sakhī,* in His hands. He will never abandon it; it always remains with Him. Sometimes for increasing the waves of *līlā* and for the pleasure of the *gopīs*, He enters a *kuñja* and "falls asleep". Knowingly He allows the flute to hang loosely in His hand – He is not really sleeping. And seeing Him from a hidden position and thinking that He is sleeping, the *gopīs* say, "Now we should take the flute!"

Then Rādhikā says to the other *gopīs*, "Who is prepared to do it? If He awakens He will grab you!" Then everyone becomes afraid. In pretending to be asleep, Kṛṣṇa certainly has some special intention. If there is any person who can take the flute, it is Rādhikā. All the *gopīs* propose that She do it, and She agrees. Smiling and watching Him very carefully, She approaches stealthily like a cat. Standing over Him, She looks carefully to see if He is really sleeping; then She snatches the flute and quickly departs the *kuñja*. Then Kuṇḍalatā comes and scolds Kṛṣṇa, "Your everything is gone, and You are sleeping?" Getting up and looking around, Kṛṣṇa says, "Hey! Where has My flute gone?" Very perturbed He says, "Who took it? Did you see who took it?" Then He approaches the *gopīs*, and as if He knows nothing, says, "Have you seen My flute?" In this way He knowingly allows the flute to be taken in order to taste some special *rasa*; otherwise He would never abandon it. In the *Brahma-saṁhitā* it says that the flute is His dearmost companion. The vibration of this flute can melt anything, even rugged mountains, and it is also capable of entering devotees' bodies and stealing their hearts. If the flute were not there, then so many of His pastimes (*līlā*) and sportive merriment (*vilāsa*) would be meaningless; such is the importance of the flute. Being held to His lips it drinks the *rasa* there and becomes intoxicated, inspiring the *gopīs* to say in the *Veṇu-gīta*, "This inanimate stick of bamboo is relishing that which is our property – the nectar of Your lips!"

In the verse we are explaining here, the name Devakī-suta has been used. Once, Devakī-suta, Dvārakādhīśa, went to the heavenly planets; Vrajendra-nandana Kṛṣṇa didn't go there. Dvārakādhīśa went there to acquire the *pārijāta* flower to appease the heart of Satyabhāmā, and approaching Indra, He said, "Dear brother, you are always very affectionate towards Me; therefore please give Me one *pārijāta* flower." When Indra refused to give Him even one flower, Kṛṣṇa uprooted the entire tree, and sitting along with Satyabhāmā on the back of His carrier Garuḍa, prepared to leave there. Indra and the demigods tried to stop Him, and after defeating them He returned to Dvārakā and planted the beautiful *pārijāta* tree in Satyabhāmā's garden. This was Devakī-suta, Dvārakādhīśa-Kṛṣṇa, who bestowed the touch of His feet on the heavenly planets, but there you won't find peacocks dancing. He doesn't play the flute there; if there is anything to be found in His hands there, it will be the conchshell and disc. He didn't play the flute there or exhibit the four special aspects of sweetness that are found only in Vṛndāvana. Therefore the fame of Vraja is greater than that of the heavenly planets, Vaikuṇṭha or Dvārakā.

In Vaikuṇṭha, Lakṣmī receives the touch of Nārāyaṇa's feet. Nārāyaṇa is an extension of Kṛṣṇa who possesses all six opulences, but the four kinds of *mādhurī* are not present in Vaikuṇṭha. There you won't find the peacocks dancing to the melody of the flute. Therefore when the word *devakī* is used in this verse, we can understand it to be another name for Yaśodā, because it is Vṛndāvana-Kṛṣṇa, or Govinda, who played the flute. And when He played the flute, all living entities forgot their normal course of activities and stood silently and motionless, listening. How did the *gopīs* hear the flute and witness the dancing of the peacocks? Sitting in their homes, they heard and saw it all in meditation. They said, "Look! The peacocks are descending to the meadow to dance to the melody of Kṛṣṇa's flute, but can *we* go there? We also desire to sing and dance with Him, but there are so many restrictions upon us. Our elders are watching over us, so it is not possible for us. Therefore we are greatly unfortunate."

Chapter Three

The Best Servant of Hari

In the next verse the *gopīs* glorify Govardhana Hill, which is not only the crown of Vṛndāvana, but the crown of the entire universe.

hantāyam adrir abalā hari-dāsa-varyo
yad-rāma-kṛṣṇa-caraṇa-sparaśa-pramodaḥ
mānaṁ tanoti saha-go-gaṇayos tayor yat
pānīya-sūyavasa-kandara-kandamūlaiḥ

Śrīmad-Bhāgavatam (10.21.18); *Bṛhad-bhāgavatāmṛta* (2.7.109)

This Govardhana Hill is the best of all those who are known as *hari-dāsa* because he is feeling great jubilation from the touch of the lotus feet of Kṛṣṇa and Balarāma. With great respect Govardhana is worshipping them by providing all their necessities such as caves, fruits, flowers and water for their pleasure, and for the pleasure of their cowherd friends, cows and calves.

Vṛndāvana is glorious because there Kṛṣṇa is playing the flute in the meadows of Govardhana and the peacocks are dancing, and becoming stunned, all of the birds and animals are listening and watching. The *gopīs* say *hantāyam*, which means they are expressing their feelings of sorrow, yet there is so much *ānanda* in it. They are disappointed because they cannot have *darśana* of Kṛṣṇa and externally join in the festivities, yet they are feeling increasing ecstasy as they experience it all internally within their meditation. "We are *abalā*, devoid of strength. Why? The female deer go near Kṛṣṇa with their husbands following behind them, and there is nothing in this world to restrict them. But for us, *everyone* is an obstacle – our husbands, mothers-in-law, fathers-in-law, brothers and friends. And what is the greatest obstacle of all? The restrictions that exist in our own minds: our fear of being disgraced in society. Therefore we are *abalā*."

Prema-bhakti is something that is *anugatya* – without the mercy of the spiritual master, it can never be attained.

śrī-guru-caraṇa-padma, kevala-bhakati-sadma,
vando mui sāvadhāna-mate

The lotus feet of the *guru* are the *sadma*, the shelter, for that *śrī*, the *prema-bhakti* for Kṛṣṇa, which exists in the heart of that *guru*. This is its source. If one does not have devotion for the spiritual master, does not serve him and is not surrendered to him in all respects, then *bhakti* will never come. Unless one attains his mercy, one will never experience *bhakti* and will never receive *darśana* of Kṛṣṇa. Therefore here the *gopīs* are saying, "*Sakhī*, for a long time we have been desiring to meet with Kṛṣṇa, but our feet are unable to go there, our eyes are unable to see Him and our hands are unable to touch Him. In our helpless condition we cannot attain His *darśana*. The birds and the deer and everyone else is allowed to receive His touch and serve Him, but we are not. However, nearby is Girirāja, who is *hari-dāsa-varya* – the best servant of Hari – and he is *guru*. If we surrender to him, if we go to him and offer *pūjā* to him and serve him, then certainly we will receive the good opportunity to serve Kṛṣṇa." This is the nature of the spiritual master:

sākṣād-dharitvena samasta-śāstrair
uktas tathā bhāvyata eva sadbhiḥ
kintu prabhor yaḥ priya eva tasya
vande guroḥ śrī-caraṇāravindam

Śrī Gurvaṣṭaka (7)

The *guru* is the one who is especially dear to Kṛṣṇa. All *jīvas* are dear to Him, yet by serving and receiving the mercy of such a *guru* who can actually overpower Kṛṣṇa by *prema*, we can meet Him; otherwise we can't meet Him. All devotees performing circumambulation (*parikramā*) of Govardhana should visit the temple of Harideva. If one performs the entire Govardhana *parikramā* without first taking *darśana* of Harideva, then he will not receive the full benefit of his *parikramā*. So the *gopīs* are saying, "On the pretext of bathing in Mānasī-gaṅgā, we will first take *darśana* of Harideva, and then we will go to Girirāja-Govardhana, where the desires of our hearts will be completely fulfilled. Our desires will be completely fulfilled because somewhere on top of Govardhana, Kṛṣṇa is taking the cows to graze and playing with His friends. There we will be able to receive His *darśana*, to receive His touch and to freely mix with Him – this is the main objective of our lives."

This should also be the main objective of *our* lives. Meeting Kṛṣṇa and attaining Kṛṣṇa's service – solely for this purpose we are practising *sādhana*. Ultimately the *sādhana* (practice) and *sādhya* (goal) of *bhakti* are one and the same. For instance there is *śravaṇa*, hearing – what will we hear? The science of the Supreme Lord (*bhagavat-tattva*), and especially the nature of the illusory nergy (*māyā-tattva*) we must understand well: "That which we are seeing now and which we are attached to due to our selfishness will only bring us unhappiness." Until we surrender to the feet of the spiritual master and follow the *sādhana* that he prescribes, we are just following the advice given to us by our own minds. When we take exclusive shelter of the *guru*, he will save us from our own independence. Then we should empty our hearts completely and accept the spiritual master's order and act accordingly. We must make our hearts one with *guru* and the Vaiṣṇavas, and one with our previous *ācāryas* like Śrīla

Viśvanātha Cakravartī Ṭhākura, Śrīla Bhaktivinoda Ṭhākura and Śrīla Bhaktisiddhānta Sarasvatī Prabhupāda. If we keep our hearts separate from them, then *māyā* will certainly snatch us. If we don't surrender our independence to them, then we will only act according to our own desire. We should depend solely on them: "As they instruct me, I will do. I will apply all of my intelligence to carrying out their orders." Then we will be successful; otherwise *bhakti*, which is fully spiritual and has its own independent nature, will not come easily.

Therefore here the *gopīs* are saying, "By thousands of our own efforts we will never overcome the obstacles that prevent us from meeting Kṛṣṇa, such as fear of our elders and adherence to the regulations of *varṇāśrama-dharma*. They will only be overcome when we attain the mercy of Girirāja." And those of us in the stage of *sādhana* should never leave the company of that Vaiṣṇava who is actually qualified to be followed. So many distractions may come, but we should never leave him – this is instruction number one. According to his desire we will move, and then we will surely progress upwards in the kingdom of *bhajana*. But if we listen instead to the dictates of our minds, we will descend into the hell known as Rasātala. What kind of things does the mind tell us? "Look, take good care of your body. Remain comfortable, and endeavour only for that happiness which is easily obtained." And following these instructions we will become trapped in the reactions to our enjoyment, and suffer. Therefore instead we should honour the instructions of the spiritual master, the Vaiṣṇavas and the scriptures. Like the *gopīs* are saying in this verse, we are *abalā* – we have no vitality in our association with *sādhus*. If we are living in a temple but we never speak to anyone, and we don't have love for both the *guru* and other Vaiṣṇavas, then what will happen? We will become isolated and discouraged. Lovingly we should speak with them, ask questions, attentively listen to the answers, and have a mood of affectionate reciprocation with them in all respects. Without them, we are *abalā* – we have no spiritual strength.

prācīnānāṁ bhajanam atulaṁ duṣkaraṁ sṛṇvato me
nairāśyena jvalati hṛdayaṁ bhakti-leśālasasya

Stava-mālā

How did previous great personalities obtain their most cherished objectives? For sixty thousand years Kaśyapa Ṛṣi and Aditi stood on their hands and went without eating, drinking and even breathing. After they performed such severe austerities, Nārāyaṇa appeared and offered them a boon. Kaśyapa Ṛṣi said, "We desire a son like you, we desire a son like you, we desire a son like you." Nārāyaṇa replied, "Where will you get a son like me? Therefore I myself will come as your son." And because he had asked three times, Nārāyaṇa became their son in three separate births. We can see what severe austerities Hiraṇyakaśipu performed to obtain only material things. For acquiring his own planet, Dhruva Mahārāja performed very severe austerities. Someone offered Sanātana Gosvāmī a quilt, but fearing that it may make him sleep more, he said, "Burn it!" But on the contrary, what are we doing? With great pleasure all day we are eating, sleeping, joking, laughing, quarrelling and in the midst of all this we chant a little *harināma*. Relatively easily we can rid ourselves of our worldly attachments, but that rare *prema* which we are aspiring for will not come if we are going on like this. We must have great eagerness, always thinking, "How will I meet Kṛṣṇa?"

Once Bhagavān gave Nārada his *darśana* and then immediately disappeared, and Nārada began crying profusely. Why did he disappear? "Inside you there is not sufficient eagerness; therefore I have come to increase your eagerness for attaining my association. In your present form you cannot always remain with me, but when your eagerness to be with me becomes sufficiently intense, you will automatically shed your present body, and then you will always be able to see me." But our *bhajana* is not filled with eagerness and intensity. If our hearts are not completely melted we will never meet Kṛṣṇa, so there is only one hope: "We are standing on the shores of the ocean of Your kindness, and if even one drop of that ocean falls upon us, then our lives will become meaningful." Our only hope is that sometime or other we will meet Him.

Therefore if we are fortunate enough to acquire the company of a real Vaiṣṇava, we should stay with him and adopt his ways, hoping that one day we will receive the direct mercy of Kṛṣṇa. The *gopīs* are saying, "We are *abalā* because our feet are unable to take us to Kṛṣṇa. Thousands of people will see us and say, 'Where are you going?' Or they will say to our parents, 'Where is your daughter going? She has become a disgrace to your family!'" It is like this in modern times also when a family member begins to engage in *bhajana*. If a son or daughter drinks and smokes, goes to the cinema, and keeps illicit connections with the opposite sex, then the family members think nothing of it. But if someone leaves everything for *bhajana*, they say that he or she has become a disgrace to the family. If a *sādhu* hears about this, what will *he* say? "Because he has taken up *bhajana*, he has become the lamp-light of the family." And hearing of this, that person's forefathers, whether they are in Pitṛloka or wherever, will begin dancing: "Now a devotee has appeared in our family!"

The *gopīs* are saying *hari-dāsa-varyaḥ* – Govardhana is the best servant of Hari. He in whom Kṛṣṇa invests all of His good qualities is called a devotee of Bhagavān, and that person is *hari-dāsa*. Three personalities have been referred to as *hari-dāsa*: Yudhiṣṭhira Mahārāja, Śrī Uddhava and Girirāja-Govardhana. Yudhiṣṭhira Mahārāja has three types of relationships with Kṛṣṇa: in *vātsalya-bhāva*, *sakhya-bhāva* and *dāsya-bhāva*. He serves Kṛṣṇa in these three sentiments, according to the necessity. He loves Kṛṣṇa in the same way as he does Arjuna and Sahadeva, as a younger brother. As Kṛṣṇa's friend he jokes and laughs with Him. And by considering that everything he possesses – his kingdom, wealth, wife, sons – is for the service of Kṛṣṇa, he acts as His servant. After Kṛṣṇa had left Hastināpura, Yudhiṣṭhira Mahārāja felt that his kingdom no longer had any value, but as long as Kṛṣṇa was present there, he felt that all of his property was for the service of Kṛṣṇa. Whenever Kṛṣṇa desired to leave there and go to Dvārakā, Yudhiṣṭhira Mahārāja would approach Kuntī and say, "My dear mother, He will not listen to me, but He will listen to you. Please speak with Him." To Draupadī he would say, "He won't listen to me, so you just let some tears fall from your eyes. He won't listen to me because I won't cry, but by crying a little you will capture Him." Then because she started crying, and Kuntī cried also, Kṛṣṇa would not go. In this way, sometimes implementing some trickery, he would serve Kṛṣṇa. Even *rasika* Vaiṣṇavas like Nārada pray to Yudhiṣṭhira Mahārāja, "You are *hari-dāsa.* Accompanied by His queens, Kṛṣṇa comes to your palace, and so many *sādhus* also come. The *sādhus* come because they want to experience the glories of Kṛṣṇa, but I have not come for that reason. I have come for *your darśana*; your *prema* is so elevated that it even overpowers Kṛṣṇa."

Uddhava is Kṛṣṇa's minister, friend and servant, and he even performed the function of a *priya-narma-sakhā* when he delivered a message from Kṛṣṇa to the *gopīs.* There is *pūrṇa* (complete), which is Yudhiṣṭhira Mahārāja, *pūrṇatara* (more complete), which is Uddhava, and *pūrṇatama* (most complete), which is Girirāja-Govardhana. In whichever *rasa* Kṛṣṇa desires to enjoy, Girirāja-Govardhana is ready to serve Him. In the *śānta-*, *dāsya-*, *sakhya-*, *vātsalya-*, *mādhurya-* and *sumādhurya-rasas*, Govardhana makes the suitable arrangement for Kṛṣṇa, and is therefore known as the best of those who are *hari-dāsa*. Knowing this, the *gopīs* are saying here, "We will go to Girirāja, offer *pūjā* to Him and serve Him, and then we will attain *darśana* of Kṛṣṇa taking the cows out to graze."

In his commentary on this verse, Sanātana Gosvāmī explains that the *gopīs* were thinking, "We have no strength when it comes to tolerating all of the obstacles that prevent us from meeting Kṛṣṇa. We are sitting in our homes, and if any other disturbance comes, we can hold our patience; but for meeting Kṛṣṇa we cannot hold our patience. But if we were to abandon it, what would happen? All would be destroyed for us. We know that Kṛṣṇa has taken the cows out to graze, yet for us to go there would not be proper. If we were to go, then our mothers-in-law, fathers-in-law and all the people of the village would criticise us. Therefore we are holding our patience. If we have any hope of ever receiving the company of Kṛṣṇa, our fear of being disgraced in society, our fear of our elders, and our fear of transgressing our *dharma* must remain. Therefore we are *abalā* – we cannot abandon our patience; we don't possess the strength to do it. We are unable to go there."

In this world also these considerations exist. One would be afraid of the reaction in society if he were to leave his home, wife, children and job to engage in *bhajana*. In our *kṛṣṇa-bhajana, our* lack of strength is also an obstacle. We are very lazy, and we are always thinking of our bodily comfort. And especially those who are householders have so many responsibilities to society and to their families that obstruct them.

Soon after taking birth, Śukadeva Gosvāmī left his home and entered the jungle. His father Vyāsadeva was left crying, "My dear son! My dear son!" but Śukadeva didn't answer him. Who answered him? Only the echo of the forest; his call didn't even reach his son's ears. If not today, then tomorrow or the next day our eagerness for *kṛṣṇa-bhajana* should be like Śukadeva's, and then all of our *abalā* sentiments will go far away. When we really desire to overcome all of the obstacles to our *bhajana*, where will we get the strength to do so? The *gopīs* are saying, "For this we will go to Girirāja-Govardhana, because He is the best servant of Hari. Why? Because He doesn't just serve Kṛṣṇa, but *mānaṁ tanoti saha-go-gaṇayos tayor yat* – Kṛṣṇa has so many companions, and he serves all of them as well. He provides pure and fragrant water for the cows and *sakhās* to drink, and for washing Kṛṣṇa's feet."

By providing all necessities, Girirāja-Govardhana would offer respect not only to Kṛṣṇa, but to His companions as well. Many people are engaged in serving the spiritual master, but few offer respect to the servants of the *guru*; but when one performs the service of respecting the *guru's* servants, the *guru* is even more pleased. Similarly many devotees are serving Kṛṣṇa, but if someone serves Kṛṣṇa's devotees and pleases them, then automatically Kṛṣṇa will be pleased. Govardhana not only provides pure water, but beautiful, soft grass as well. Eating this grass, the cows become strong and give ample milk which satisfies Kṛṣṇa. And for the *sakhās* Govardhana provides not only water, but all kinds of fruits, which simply upon being seen increase their happiness: bananas, lemons, pomegranates, coconut and *tāla*, which is especially fragrant.

Govardhana also provided caves for the *sakhās* when they became tired from tending the cows. On hot days the caves would be cooling, and on cold days they gave warmth, and within these caves were *kuñjas* with mirrors composed of jewels where one could see his reflection. All materials for decorating oneself and others were available there, and in this way it also became a meeting place for Kṛṣṇa and the *gopīs*. Nearby are such places as Dānaghāṭī and Dāna-nivartana-kuṇḍa, where Kṛṣṇa and Rādhikā and Her *sakhīs* took taxes from one another. So the *gopīs* are praying,

"O Girirāja-Govardhana, You are a witness to all of Kṛṣṇa's pastimes; please give us a place from where we can also witness His pastimes."

Hearing these words of the *gopīs*, a *sādhaka's* hankering will increase and he will think, "When will such a day be mine, when I can go to Girirāja-Govardhana with these sentiments of the *gopīs* flowing in my heart? I also desire to witness Kṛṣṇa's pastimes during the day." This desire is the aim and objective of our lives, and the very pinnacle of *bhajana*.

Chapter Four

The Clouds, Rivers and Trees Serve Kṛṣṇa

If someone is inimical to Bhagavān, then they will have to undergo much suffering and be very unhappy. They will have to take millions of births in the material world, and will never attain happiness in any birth. The *jīva* is a part of Bhagavān; his very intrinsic form is as a servant of Bhagavān. Abandoning this understanding, the living entity becomes opposed to Bhagavān and thinks, "I am the enjoyer of this world," "I am the master of everything," and "Everything has been created for my enjoyment." This is the illusion of the opposed *jīva*. When Kṛṣṇa disappeared from the vision of the *gopīs*, in divine madness they went searching for Him. In reality He is never far away from them; but on the contrary we have made ourselves separate from Him. If in our search for Bhagavān we have the same kind of eagerness that the *gopīs* have, then we can meet Him. But without such eagerness, we will never meet Him.

The *gopīs* possess an extremely intense eagerness to meet Kṛṣṇa, and if even a fraction of that arises within us, then it can be said that we are really searching for Kṛṣṇa in our *sādhana-bhajana*. But from where will this eagerness come? Kṛṣṇa and Śrīmatī Rādhikā both assume forms that are easily accessible to conditioned souls. For the purpose of bringing *jīvas* towards Himself, Kṛṣṇa has become the *śālagrāma-śilā*, and His dearest one has become *tulasī*. Kṛṣṇa has also entered this world in the form of Girirāja-Govardhana, and His dearest one has come in the form of the Yamunā. We can see how merciful Bhagavān is: so much so that He has made the arrangement for everyone to attain Him. Govardhana is accessible for everyone, and is fully capable of bestowing *kṛṣṇa-prema*. It has been said that he fulfils whatever desires people approach him with, and in this way has arranged a very nice trap for them. If anyone desires a son, wealth, to get their son or daughter married, a better job or whatever, they can go to Govardhana, beg from him, and he will bestow those things. In this way, at first he slowly captures people by grabbing the end of their finger, and then he grabs the whole finger, next the hand, and finally he grabs everything.

Those of you who have travelled on the trains in India have seen how they are very crowded and how no seats are available. So after boarding the train people first move near a bench, then place their hand down on it, then spread their hand out a little, and then begin to edge their way in until they have squeezed themselves into a seat. In the same way, Girirāja, the spiritual master and the Vaiṣṇavas gradually bring the conditioned soul towards *bhakti*.

Having become separated from Kṛṣṇa, the *gopīs* are thinking, "Kṛṣṇa is everything to us, so how will we meet Him? We must get the mercy of a Vaiṣṇava, and who are the best Vaiṣṇavas? Yudhiṣṭhira, Uddhava and Girirāja-Govardhana; and amongst them, Girirāja is the best. Going to Yudhiṣṭhira or Uddhava won't be fruitful; they cannot give us what we desire. Only Girirāja can give it." In this way, if we really feel that Bhagavān is our only necessity, we will have such eagerness. Then our eagerness will lead us to ask a Vaiṣṇava, "How can we meet Kṛṣṇa? How can we overcome all of our despair?" This is where we recognise our necessity for a *guru*. For obtaining any material object a *guru* is not necessary, but in spiritual matters approaching a *guru* is necessary. Girirāja will give mercy, Yamunā-devī will give mercy, Vṛndāvana-dhāma will give mercy, and we should pray to all of them.

Here the *gopīs*, through the eyes of *vipralambha-bhāva* in separation from Kṛṣṇa, are seeing *prema* in all the residents of Vṛndāvana but themselves. This is the symptom of an *uttama-adhikārī* Vaiṣṇava. There are three levels of Vaiṣṇava. The first is the *kaniṣṭha-adhikārī*, and his symptoms are that even though he offers *pūjā* to the deity and accepts that the water of holy places and the water that has washed the deity is sacred, he does not detect the presence of Bhagavān within the hearts of other living entities. He considers the body to be the self, and has no respect for the devotees of Bhagavān. He doesn't believe that the spiritual master knows all; he thinks that the *guru* may possess more knowledge than he does, but that he certainly doesn't know everything. Therefore he feels that there is no real necessity of taking advice from the *guru*. Upon not obtaining the material things that he desires from his practice of *bhajana*, he may become disgusted and even abandon his *bhajana*.

The symptoms of the *madhyama-adhikārī* Vaiṣṇava have been told to be that he has love for Bhagavān, he has friendship with other devotees, he is merciful to those who are faithful and he remains indifferent towards those who are opposed to Bhagavān. He wants to give mercy to everyone, but it is not possible to love everyone; it is inappropriate. One cannot show love to a snake or a tiger – they will only attack you. Therefore he behaves suitably towards others according to their qualification.

The *uttama-adhikārī* Vaiṣṇava sees the presence of his master in the hearts of all *jīvas*, and believes that they all have the same feelings for Bhagavān that he does. Prahlāda Mahārāja saw that his worshipful deity was in the hearts of all living entities, and that even the trees had the same feelings of *śānta-* and *dāsya-rasa* towards Bhagavān that he did. Similarly the *gopīs* saw their own sentiments sometimes within Girirāja, sometimes within the deer of Vṛndāvana and sometimes even within the clouds. And they also saw that just as Kṛṣṇa loves them, He also loves all the other residents of Vṛndāvana in the same way. Therefore the *uttama-adhikārī* doesn't see anywhere in the world a living entity who is not engaged in *bhajana* and who doesn't have the same sentiment for Kṛṣṇa as he himself does.

mama vartmānuvartante
manuṣyāḥ pārtha sarvaśaḥ

Bhagavad-gītā (4.11)

Everyone follows My path in all respects, O son of Pṛthā.

The highest devotees *really* see that everyone is serving Bhagavān – don't think that this statement is an exaggeration. The *gopīs* actually see that, "Just as we love Kṛṣṇa, all of the trees, creepers, birds, mountains and rivers of Vṛndāvana are fully conscious and are serving Kṛṣṇa." They are planning to go to Govardhana on the pretext of going to bathe in Mānasī-gaṅgā and having *darśana* of Harideva because nearby there, Kṛṣṇa is taking the cows out to graze, and then they will surely receive His *darśana*. In this way, with his eyes closed and chanting the holy name, an *uttama-adhikārī* similarly meditates on the pastimes of Kṛṣṇa, especially His eternal eightfold daily pastimes (*aṣṭakāla-līlā*). Meditating more and more, eventually the object of his meditation appears to him, and he becomes absorbed in that flow: "I am at Govardhana, and I am doing my service." When his vision begins to dissipate, he begins to lament, "*Hāya! Hāya!*" And here, as the day progresses and the *gopīs* are sitting in their homes and conversing, their absorption in the previous *bhāva* begins to diminish, and one *sakhī* says to Rādhikā:

dṛṣṭvātape vraja-paśūn saha rāma-gopaiḥ
sañcārayantam anu veṇum udīrayantam
prema-pravṛddha uditaḥ kusumāvalībhiḥ
sakhyur vyadhāt sva-vapuṣāmbuda ātapatram

Śrīmad-Bhāgavatam (10.21.16); *Bṛhad-bhāgavatāmṛta* (2.7.110)

Seeing Kṛṣṇa and Balarāma playing their flutes in the afternoon sun and taking the cows and calves out for grazing, the clouds burst with divine love, and like an umbrella shield their friend Śrī Kṛṣṇa from the sun while showering tiny drops of rain that are like a shower of flowers.

Now it is afternoon time, and taking the cows out to graze accompanied by Baladeva and the *gopas*, Kṛṣṇa has entered the forest. Desiring fresh grass to eat, the cows grazed on and on until they reached the rocks of Govardhana. The rocks were very hot in the afternoon sun, and the sand and soil below their feet were also very hot. Thinking that the cows and His friends were feeling some pain due to this, Kṛṣṇa played the flute in such a way that at once the clouds gathered and began to shower soft rain.

In India there are many *rāgas* that are well-known for producing different effects. Once there was a *guru* named Haridāsajī who was a master of *rāgas*, and he had two disciples named Baijubāvara and Tanasena. Tanasena was a singer in the court of the king, and it was his policy that if anyone came to Delhi to sing, they were obligated to challenge him in the royal court – and if they were defeated, they would have to face punishment from the king. Hearing of this, Baijubāvara went to Delhi and began skilfully singing different melodies, and a large crowd of people gathered to hear him. The news of this reached the king, who said, "Who is this person daring to sing here? This is a great insult to Tanasena!" So he called for Baijubāvara and said to him, "You must have the proper qualification; otherwise you are not allowed to sing in Delhi."

Baijubāvara said, "All right, we will have a competition. Where will it be held?"

"It will be held in the royal assembly."

"Then who will decide the winner? Who will decide whose singing is the sweetest and the most beautiful?"

"All of my queens here will decide."

"No, I can't trust them. I want the animals of the jungle to make the decision, and then I will accept it. The queens will all certainly be prejudiced. Therefore we should go to the jungle and see whose singing pleases the animals most."

"All right, so it shall be."

The entire assembly went to the jungle, and first Tanasena sang. Then Baijubāvara sang, and groups of deer immediately gathered there. These deer became so absorbed in his singing that he reached over and placed a flower garland around the neck of one of them. Then as soon as he stopped singing, all of the deer ran off very quickly. Baijubāvara said, "If Tanasena is a better singer than me, then he should call all of these deer back with his singing, and once they are again absorbed, he should reach over and retrieve the garland." Tanasena stood and began singing, and he sang with such effort that he was perspiring heavily, but still the deer didn't come, and he couldn't retrieve the garland. Then Baijubāvara sang again, and this time even more deer came and at once again became absorbed in his singing. With one hand he reached over and took back the garland, and then when he stopped singing, all the deer ran off again. In previous times there were singers and musicians like this who could also produce effects like bringing rain or even starting a fire without the use of any matches or other such things. Therefore we can scarcely conceive of the effects Kṛṣṇa's flute-playing is capable of producing.

After entering the forest, Kṛṣṇa played the flute in such a way that it bewildered everyone, and the clouds saw that, "Our friend has come! We should show some respect to our friend." Why was there friendship between them? Because they were of the same darkish blue (*śyāma*) colour. The afternoon sun had made the rocks and the soil underfoot very hot, and when Kṛṣṇa played this particular *rāga* on the flute, wherever the *sakhās* and cows were standing they became stunned and just listened, and the clouds began to gather in groups. But they didn't only come for Kṛṣṇa: wherever there were *gopas*, cows or calves standing, the clouds desired to render service and they covered the sun with their own bodies like an umbrella. As they rendered this service, it increased their *prema*, and tears of joy came to their eyes. These tears took the form of cooling drops of rain, and they fell softly from the sky like an offering of flowers.

The *gopīs* are saying, "These clouds are so fortunate! We cannot be equal to them; we cannot render even a little service to Kṛṣṇa. No one is as unfortunate as us." *Sādhakas* should also feel like this – "Everyone is serving Kṛṣṇa, but I am not." If a *sādhaka* feels this way, then he will surely make progress in his *sādhana*. Otherwise, if he sees the faults in others, then all of those faults will in return come within him. Therefore we should never see the faults in other devotees, but should always make an effort to recognise only their good qualities.

Next comes this verse:

nadyas tadā tad upadhārya mukunda-gītam
āvarta-lakṣita-manobhava-bhagna-vegāḥ
āliṅgana-sthagitam ūrmi-bhujair murārer
gṛhṇanti pāda-yugalaṁ kamalopahārāḥ

Śrīmad-Bhāgavatam (10.21.15); *Bṛhad-bhāgavatāmṛta* (2.7.111)

O *sakhīs*, when the rivers of Vṛndāvana headed by the Yamunā hear the vibration of Kṛṣṇa's flute, their currents completely stop, and their waters begin to swirl as if they are overcome with desire. With their arms in the form of waves they reach out to touch and offer lotus flowers to His lotus feet.

These verses describe the sentiment of elevated devotees, but they may not even come to all elevated devotees; they are exclusively the sentiments of the *gopīs*. So why have they been given in the *Bhāgavatam*? These verses are there for the benefit of those *sādhakas* who have a similar type of hankering as the *gopīs* do. By remembering these verses more and more, some day, in some lifetime, this beautiful *bhāva* of the *gopīs'* eagerness to meet Kṛṣṇa will enter their hearts. As the *gopīs* are sitting in their homes, one *bhāva* arises within them, and then as it diminishes, another immediately arises. This is called *bhāva-śābalya*, where one *bhāva* is fully relished and then another comes. The meaning of this verse is that as the *gopīs* were looking towards the Yamunā, they said, "O *sakhī*, hearing the flute-song of Mukunda, the river is carrying all the lotuses like gifts in her thousands of arms and offering them as *puṣpāñjali* to Kṛṣṇa's feet. The waves of the river have stopped flowing, and a whirlpool has been created. This whirlpool is a symptom of *manobhava*, the river's love for Kṛṣṇa."

Who is the husband of the Yamunā, Mānasī-gaṅgā and the other rivers of Vraja? The ocean, because they all flow towards him. But these rivers don't flow easily towards their husband. The best of these rivers is the one who is the dearest to Bhagavān: Kālindī, she who springs forth from the Kālinda Mountain. Kālindī is the one whose water, from receiving Kṛṣṇa's touch or from the *añjana* of the *gopīs*, has assumed Kṛṣṇa's *śyāma* colour. Having had her heart stolen by the sound of Kṛṣṇa's flute, the waves of her *bhāva* were like her hands, and taking a gift of lotuses – *kamalopahārāḥ* – in these hands, she offered them to the feet of Kṛṣṇa. *Kamalopahārāḥ* can also mean Lakṣmī, which means splendour. What is the splendour of a river? The lotus; so it can also mean taking that splendour and offering it to Kṛṣṇa's feet. The waves have been said to be Kālindī's long, long arms, and there were not just two of these arms, but thousands and thousands of waves surrounding Kṛṣṇa's feet. Why? For grasping His feet so He wouldn't be able to go away from there. In this way, after offering a gift of all her splendour – the lotuses – she submerged Kṛṣṇa's feet in her waves as if grasping them, thereby placing them in her heart.

The *gopīs* are saying, "How can we go and grasp the feet of Kṛṣṇa in this way? We are very afraid of being disgraced in society, and therefore we cannot go. We are unable to abandon our present circumstances to meet with Kṛṣṇa. But this river is indicating to us, 'You are unable to do what I have done? Being attracted by Kṛṣṇa's flute you are not able to leave everything – as I have stopped flowing towards my husband, the ocean – and place all of your splendour at His feet? You do not have that much courage? You are so afraid of being disgraced in society?' But we are unable to do it, and therefore if there is anyone in this world who is unfortunate, it is us. Having taken birth in these circumstances, we are unable to meet Kṛṣṇa, to speak with Him or to serve Him, because we are always busy in our household affairs. But this river has abandoned everything, even its fierce flow, and embraced the feet of Kṛṣṇa."

It is the same for us; we are unable to engage in *sādhana-bhajana*. In the same way as the river offered the gift of lotuses to Kṛṣṇa's feet, we should offer our very hearts to the spiritual master and the Vaiṣṇavas. We may have everything – the association of *guru* and the Vaiṣṇavas – but as yet we have no such eagerness by which we can turn the tendency of our minds away from material enjoyment and exclusively towards Kṛṣṇa. This is the message being carried by the river, and the instruction being given here through the medium of the *gopīs*.

Next comes this verse:

vana-latās tarava ātmani viṣṇuṁ
vyañjayantya iva puṣpa-phalāḍhyāḥ
praṇata-bhāra-viṭapā madhu-dhārāḥ
prema-hṛṣṭa-tanavo vavṛṣuḥ sma

Śrīmad-Bhāgavatam (10.35.9); *Bṛhad-bhāgavatāmṛta* (2.7.112)

Look how the creepers and the branches of the trees of Vṛndāvana are drooping down due to their weight! They must have also taken Śrī Kṛṣṇa within their hearts, because tears of love in the form of streams of honey are dripping from them, and the emergence of their fruits and flowers bear witness to their ecstatic rapture.

The previous verses were all from the *Veṇu-gīta* of the *Śrīmad-Bhāgavatam* [chapter 21 of the Tenth Canto], but this verse is from the *Yugala-gīta* [chapter 35 of the Tenth Canto]. What is the meaning of the *Yugala-gīta*? The *gopīs* are singing to each other concerning their separation from Kṛṣṇa. In the *Veṇu-gīta* there was more *pūrva-rāga*, preliminary attraction, but here, after meeting with Kṛṣṇa, they are speaking about their agitated state of *vipralambha-bhāva*. One who has such eagerness as the *gopīs* are expressing here will be able to meet Kṛṣṇa and His dearest ones.

The system for spiritual enlightenment is arranged by Kṛṣṇa alone. Here someone may ask, "There are so many *jīvas* in the world, so are they all in *mādhurya-rasa*? There are numerous devotees performing *bhajana* in the *sampradāyas* of Nimbārka, Rāmānuja and Viṣṇusvāmī, and there are others such as *yavanas* who perform no *bhajana* at all. Why is it that they don't all come towards *mādhurya-rasa*?" The answer is that Bhagavān is so merciful that all the systems in this world are in His hands; according to a person's particular actions, a certain fruit is bestowed upon them. Every *jīva* certainly has a particular instrinsic *rasa*. Five primary sentiments have been described: *śānta*, *dāsya*, *sakhya*, *vātsalya* and *mādhurya*, and every *jīva* falls within one of these categories. Yet from time immemorial he has been taking birth, dying, sometimes attaining the higher planetary systems and then again returning here, wandering in all directions.

Those who were more fortunate took birth in Satya-yuga, where most people worshipped Bhagavān through *śānta-rasa*, as the four Kumāras and the Nara-Nārāyaṇa *ṛṣis* did. After this Śrī Rāmacandra came and emphasised the glories of *dāsya-rasa*, and for preaching this ideal, Hanumān remained in this world after the disappearance of Rāma. Then Kṛṣṇa came at the end of Dvāpara-yuga and gave *prema* even to the creepers. He performed such pastimes that simply by hearing and chanting about them, especially through the medium of *Śrīmad-Bhāgavatam*, a *jīva* could be attracted and gradually attain that *bhāva*. But there were some *jīvas* who were contemporary with Kṛṣṇa yet could not understand His pastimes. Śiśupāla, Kaṁsa, Duḥśāsana and Jarāsandha criticised this *bhāva*: "Oh, in Vraja this boy of no particular caste has appeared, no one even knows for sure who his real mother and father are, and now he has become a king in Dvārakā and will rule over us?"

In the *Bhāgavatam* it is stated that Kṛṣṇa is Svayam Bhagavān, and all *bhāvas* are included in Him, yet the *bhāva* He showed in Vraja was not shown anywhere else. But very few people outside of Vraja actually accepted that *bhāva* at that time and just criticised Him for it. For this reason Kṛṣṇa inspired Śukadeva Gosvāmī: "You please manifest the shining sun of *Śrīmad-Bhāgavatam*. No one else is capable; you are *līlā-śuka*, the expert narrator of our pastimes." Then on the pretext of Parīkṣit Mahārāja being cursed to die by the bite of a snakebird, the *Bhāgavatam* was manifest by Śukadeva Gosvāmī; but at that time very few people were actually qualified to accept it. Then Śaṅkarācārya came, then Madhva, then Rāmānuja, and other *ācāryas* came and gave *dāsya-rasa*, and maybe a little *sakhya-rasa*. Finally Caitanya Mahāprabhu came with His eternal associates, and through the medium of *Śrīmad-Bhāgavatam* validated that special *vraja-bhāva* and gave *prema* to the world. Meeting the incarnation of Bhagavān who goes by the name Vrajendra-nandana is the ideal that is being described in these verses from the *Bhāgavatam*.

The *gopīs*, being extremely agitated to meet Kṛṣṇa, have even forgotten their own bodies. Which Kṛṣṇa are they desiring? Sakhā-Kṛṣṇa, the Kṛṣṇa who is so dear to them. If anyone becomes similarly agitated to have Kṛṣṇa as their own friend, son or dear one, and goes to an elevated devotee and hears *kṛṣṇa-kathā* from him, then easily he can attain *kṛṣṇa-prema*. Otherwise there is no way to attain it; Caitanya Mahāprabhu Himself came and showed the way. And who was accompanying Him? Svarūpa Dāmodara, Rāya Rāmānanda, and Rūpa, Sanātana and Raghunātha dāsa Gosvāmīs. He bestowed all of His mercy on Svarūpa Dāmodara and Rāya Rāmānanda by relishing *kathā* with them night after night, but He invested His potency (*śakti*) directly into the hearts of Rūpa at Prayāga and Sanātana at Vārāṇasī. Through them this *bhāva* was manifest in the world, and everyone was drowned in the ocean of *bhakti-rasa*. Before the appearance of Mahāprabhu these things were not known; no one could even imagine them. Whenever Mahāprabhu saw a forest, He considered it to be Vṛndāvana, whenever He saw a body of water, He took it to be the Kālindī, and whenever He saw any elevated land, He took it to be Govardhana. This is the *bhāva* of an *uttama-adhikārī*.

So in this verse the *gopīs* are saying, "Aho! Kṛṣṇa has continued on His way playing the flute, and it seems that all of the trees, creepers and mountains of Vṛndāvana are revealing their hearts to Him. The creepers have very large flowers and the trees have very large fruits, and it seems that upon seeing Kṛṣṇa they have begun laughing in great ecstasy. The *prema* within them has manifested externally in the form of their ripening fruits and blossoming flowers. And when Kṛṣṇa passes by them, those trees and creepers bend over, and those fruits and flowers that are normally at the height of His head are offered to His feet as *puṣpāñjali*. And expressing their *prema* for Him, there is an incessant flow of streams of honey emanating from them. But we are so unfortunate; we are unable to meet Kṛṣṇa. These creepers and trees have so much *prema* for Kṛṣṇa in their hearts, and it is manifesting in the form of all the fruits and flowers and streams of honey, which are like tears flowing from their eyes. But can *we* take any fruits and flowers to Kṛṣṇa? What would people say? Because of our fear of being disgraced in society we are unable to go. But maybe if in our next lives we assume the form of trees and creepers, then we will also be able to serve Kṛṣṇa."

Chapter Five

Happiness in Separation

In appearance the trees and creepers of Vṛndāvana seem to be ordinary, but upon seeing Kṛṣṇa they became overwhelmed in *bhāva*. With great joy they offered *praṇāma* to the feet of Kṛṣṇa by offering their fruits and flowers, and they shed tears of love in the form of streams of honey. Even the plants and trees of this world have feelings; like us they are conscious. They are not able to express their feelings in words, but they can express them. Especially the trees and creepers of Vṛndāvana are all *viśuddha-sattva*, meaning that they are superior to those of us situated in mixed goodness. So what won't they understand? They can understand and experience everything. Therefore by offering their fruits and flowers in ecstatic rapture, they offered *praṇāma* to Kṛṣṇa.

In his commentary, Sanātana Gosvāmī is saying that these trees and creepers are more conscious than the clouds. The *gopīs* felt that all the other residents of Vṛndāvana were serving Kṛṣṇa, but that they themselves were not. They saw that even the clouds were serving Him by creating an umbrella above His head to block out the sun, and by showering cooling rain on Him. So the trees and creepers were even more conscious than the clouds, and we can see their condition upon hearing the vibration of Kṛṣṇa's flute and receiving His *darśana*! Concerning Śrī Caitanya Mahāprabhu, Narottama dāsa Ṭhākura wrote:

paśu-pākhī jhure, pāṣāṇa vidare,
śuni' jāṅa guṇa-gāthā

Upon witnessing the pastimes of Mahāprabhu, the birds, animals and insects would melt in divine love. When Mahāprabhu was in Ālālanātha, upon hearing His crying the stone there melted, and His footprints and imprints from where He fell unconscious were easily indented there. When Śrī Rāmacandra and Bharata met at Citrakūṭa, upon feeling the mutual love of the two brothers, the stone there melted. When Kṛṣṇa played the flute at Caraṇa-pahāḍī in Kāmyavana, the stone melted and He left fifty or more footprints there. These footprints are certainly His – they were not made by anyone else. So even stones, clouds, trees and animals can melt in emotion, but we have not yet become melted in emotion. We haven't yet developed the intense eagerness that "I will certainly engage in *kṛṣṇa-bhajana*."

In the verse we began describing in the last chapter we find the line *vana-latās taravaḥ*, meaning "the creepers and trees in the forest", but why have the creepers been mentioned before the trees? It would seem that it would be proper to mention the trees first because they are primary, and without them the creepers would have nothing to climb up. But the creepers are of the same gender as the *gopīs*, and their sentiment is similar. "These creepers are female just as we are, and men don't have as much sentiment as we do." Thinking like this, the *gopīs* first mentioned the word *latā* in this verse, and then *taravaḥ*. They say *ātmani viṣṇum*, which means "He who is pervading everything", referring to *bhakta-vātsalya* Bhagavān. *Vyañjayantyaḥ* means "revealed in a special way to this Nanda-kiśora, Yaśodā-nandana, Kṛṣṇacandra or Gopī-kānta". These creepers had a treasure hidden in their hearts, but upon hearing the sound of Kṛṣṇa's flute they immediately revealed it in the form of fruits and flowers. Bowing down to

Kṛṣṇa's feet, they offered the treasure of their hearts as *praṇāma*.

There are two ways of offering *praṇāma* to someone. Someone who has very little faith will apathetically offer *praṇāma* with his hands only one time and then leave. But someone who has strong faith will bow down and offer *praṇāma* time and again with great love and humility. He will look towards his master with great affection, desiring his blessing. The trees offered *praṇāma* to Kṛṣṇa in this way, with great *prema*. Kṛṣṇa came, they offered *praṇāma*, and even after Kṛṣṇa left they remained bowing down because there was so much *prema* in their hearts.

Being submerged in the ocean of unhappiness of separation from Kṛṣṇa, how did the *gopīs* pass the day? After cooking for Kṛṣṇa at the home of Yaśodā and seeing that Kṛṣṇa has taken the cows to the forest to graze, the *gopīs* return to their homes, and those *sakhīs* who are *svapakṣa* (belonging to Rādhikā's own group) remain with Rādhikā. When someone is happy, it seems to them that the whole day passes in one minute; so in separation from Kṛṣṇa, how will the *gopīs* manage to pass the day? It says here that they engaged in *kīrtana* – singing these verses that we are reading – but did they pass the day in happiness or unhappiness? They were remembering the pastimes of Kṛṣṇa by describing them, and were revealing their inner feelings to one another, but were they feeling happiness or unhappiness? Hearing the descriptions of His pastimes, they became absorbed and felt that they were actually seeing Him, but when the excitement from that diminished, they were plunged into the depths of despair.

For the *gopīs*, happiness and unhappiness became one ocean. It says in *Śrī Caitanya-caritāmṛta*, "*viṣāmṛta ekatra milana* – poison and nectar became one." I am not able to explain this in such a way that you will understand this, or even to fully understand it myself. Because we are presently standing on the platform of *māyā,* wrapped up in material enjoyment, we cannot understand this. Then why are we hearing of it? It is like a coating of wax. If you are placing candles here and there, then a little wax comes off on your hand and creates a coating. Similarly, if a *sādhaka* reads, hears and speaks about these topics, then certainly something will rub off: a little feeling of *bhāva* will come. Then, practising *sādhana* more and more, after some time this feeling will become so strong that it will never be interrupted.

Here the *gopīs* are mutually hearing and describing Kṛṣṇa's pastimes, and as remembrance comes, they are seeing Kṛṣṇa with the eyes of *bhāva*. It appears that they are suffering due to separation, but inside them is great happiness.

evaṁ vraja-striyo rājan
kṛṣṇa-līlānugāyatīḥ
remire 'haḥsu tac-cittās
tan-manaskā mahodayāḥ

Śrīmad-Bhāgavatam (10.35.26)

O king, during the daytime the ladies of Vraja took pleasure in continuously singing about the pastimes of Kṛṣṇa, and their hearts were fully absorbed in Him.

The ladies of Vraja had offered their hearts to Kṛṣṇa. We see in the *Gopī-gīta* [chapter 31 of the Tenth Canto of *Śrīmad-Bhāgavatam*] and in the *Veṇu-gīta* that the *gopīs* are absorbed in spiritual ecstasy: even in separation from Him they remain happy by meditating on His pastimes. Yet in another place it is written that being very unhappy, they passed the day singing about His pastimes. They took shelter of only one thing – singing about Kṛṣṇa's pastimes – otherwise they would have been unable to pass the day. So are the *gopīs happy* as they sing about His pastimes, or *unhappy*? It is harmonised in this way: if we see a person really crying and wailing in separation from Kṛṣṇa, just as Śrī Caitanya Mahāprabhu did, what feelings will arise within us? Will we think that, "I never want to be like this!"? Rather we will think that if even a small fraction of that *bhāva* enters us, our lives will be completely successful. As peculiar as it seems, we actually *desire* to cry in this way. The verses in the *Bhāgavatam* describing the crying of the *gopīs* will be those most read by a *rasika* devotee. In the *Bhramara-gīta* [chapter 47 of the Tenth Canto of *Śrīmad-Bhāgavatam*] the *gopīs* are in *vipralambha-bhāva*, and speaking to a bumblebee they are expressing their suffering. It is a very sad thing, but devotees enjoy it very much.

The *Veṇu-gīta*, *Gopī-gīta*, *Yugala-gīta*, and other chapters in the *Bhāgavatam* all focus entirely on the topic of separation from Kṛṣṇa. Devotees find all of this tasteful, even though they are crying; they like crying also. Therefore here happiness is included within crying, and the *gopīs* are described in this verse as *mahodayāḥ* – experiencing a grand festival. Singing about Kṛṣṇa's pastimes during the day, they were supremely happy. Meeting Kṛṣṇa at night they were fully gratified, and in meditation during the day their minds raced after Him as He wandered in the forest. *This* is the meaning of *bhajana*. If a devotee is absorbed in meditation on *kṛṣṇa-līlā*, then that meditation *is bhajana*. "How will I meet Kṛṣṇa? So many lives have passed, and still I have not found Him."

Although externally that *prema* appears to be unhappiness, inside their meditation is immeasurable happiness. When Kṛṣṇa leaves Vṛndāvana and goes to Mathurā or Dvārakā, and at Nandagrāma or Uddhava-kyārī the *gopīs* are crying in sadness, why won't they abandon their meditation on Kṛṣṇa? Are they able to abandon it? Sūrya dāsa has written that the *gopīs* placed Kṛṣṇa's foot-dust all over their *sārīs* and their limbs, and when the tears related to Kṛṣṇa fell from their eyes and mixed with that, they became very dirty; but would any of them change their *sārīs*? So this meditation is actually full of happiness, but yes, externally it seems to be unhappiness. It is written in *Śrī Caitanya-caritāmṛta* that the happiness felt by one person meeting Kṛṣṇa exceeds the happiness felt by the residents of millions of material universes combined, and the unhappiness felt by the residents of Vṛndāvana exceeds the pain caused by the most potent poison. Therefore Sanātana Gosvāmī, Jīva Gosvāmī and Viśvanātha Cakravartī Ṭhākura have written in their commentaries that in this state of separation, happiness and unhappiness are the same.

At the end of his explanation of this verse, Sanātana Gosvāmī says that in this way Kṛṣṇa is the very embodiment of the topmost ecstasy (*paramānanda*): He is the very embodiment of *rasa*, He is the possessor of all potencies, He is all-pervading, He knows the minds and hearts of all, and He is the foundation of all *rasa*. He is both the *rasa* itself and the taster of *rasa*. He performs pastimes that establish Him as the very embodiment of *paramānanda*. There is no difference between Kṛṣṇa and His pastimes, just as there is no difference between Kṛṣṇa and His name. Being merciful, when *kṛṣṇa-līlā* sees that there is *bhāva* in our hearts, then it will appear to us. By thousands of our own efforts it will not appear, but when it is merciful to us, at that moment it will appear of its own accord.

Just as Kṛṣṇa is supremely independent, His *līlā* is also supremely independent. It will know if a recipient is qualified or not. If it sees that one's prayer is full of humility, then no matter what one's qualification may be, it will appear. It may appear in the hearts of qualified people like the four Kumāras, or in someone with a sinful background like Bilvamaṅgala. *Līlā* manifested in his heart and Kṛṣṇa Himself came to help him walk to Vraja and to listen to his sweet singing. Therefore Sanātana Gosvāmī is saying that just as Kṛṣṇa is the very embodiment of the supreme spiritual ecstasy, so are His pastimes. If one is simply hearing narrations of *kṛṣṇa-līlā*, then for him there is no necessity of practising renunciation or anything of the kind.

jñāne prayāsam udapāsya namanta eva
jīvanti san-mukharitāṁ bhavadīya-vārtām
sthāne sthitāḥ śruti-gatāṁ tanu-vāṅ-manobhir
ye prāyaśo 'jita jito 'py asi tais tri-lokyām

Śrīmad-Bhāgavatam (10.14.3)

Bhagavān is unconquerable by anyone within this world. Yet if someone faithfully hears *hari-kathā*, even while remaining within his established social position, then the disease of lust and all impediments to spiritual advancement (*anarthas*) will vanish from his heart and he will overpower that unconquerable Bhagavān – such is the potency of *līlā-kathā*. But since this *līlā-kathā* is the very embodiment of the topmost spiritual ecstasy (*paramānanda*), then what necessity will the *gopīs* feel to meet Kṛṣṇa? Won't they be satisfied just by this? They won't be satisfied. Why? Sanātana Gosvāmī gives his opinion that although Kṛṣṇa and the narrations of His pastimes are one, the *gopīs* won't be satisfied by just engaging in *līlā-kathā*. Their *prema* is such that it can never be restricted in any way, and they will never be fully pleased, fully satisfied or receive the full taste from only engaging in *līlā-kathā* without meeting Kṛṣṇa. They desire to enter directly into pastimes where Kṛṣṇa will express similar sentiments towards them as He did in the *rāsa-līlā*.

Hari-kathā by itself won't satisfy the *gopīs*, but a *sādhaka* should always continue hearing narrations of the Lord's pastimes, understanding that the unhappiness which the *gopīs* experienced while engaged in *hari-kathā* was merely a manifestation of their indescribable happiness. It is written that when *līlā-kathā* enters the ears of a *sādhaka*, it enters his heart, snatches away all inauspiciousness and makes his heart completely pure. Then it takes him to the place where he can relish a life of serving Rādhā and Kṛṣṇa with the *sakhās* and *sakhīs*; in this way Kṛṣṇa and the narrations of His pastimes are supremely merciful.

Next comes this verse:

ete 'linas tava yaśo 'khila-loka-tīrthaṁ
gāyanta ādi-puruṣānupathaṁ bhajante
prāyo amī muni-gaṇā bhavadīya-mukhyā
gūḍhaṁ vane 'pi na jahaty anaghātma-daivam

Śrīmad-Bhāgavatam (10.15.6); *Bṛhad-bhāgavatāmṛta* (2.7.113)

[Śrī Kṛṣṇa said to Balarāma:] O Ādi-puruṣa, although you are keeping your opulences hidden and are performing pastimes as a young boy here in Vṛndāvana, still the sages, who are among the best of your devotees, have recognised you. Not wanting to be separated from you for even one moment, they have assumed the forms of bees and are worshipping you by constantly singing your glories as the purifier of this world.

Kṛṣṇa and Baladeva Prabhu have taken the cows out for grazing, and using the presence of Baladeva as a pretext, Kṛṣṇa is actually praising Himself in His speaking of this verse. Here He praises Baladeva as being *ādi-puruṣa*, the original personality in all of existence, but that is actually Kṛṣṇa Himself. He is describing so many of the glories of Baladeva here, but they are actually His own glories. He says, "The buzzing of the bees in this forest is actually the chanting of Vedic *mantras*. The bees are actually *munis*, but in the form of bees they are glorifying you with poems and prayers as they follow you along. You are wearing a *vaijayantī-mālā* that is comprised of many different kinds of flowers and *tulasī* buds also. There is nectar within these buds, so sometimes these bees are sitting on the buds, sometimes on the other flowers of the garland, and sometimes they are swarming around you offering prayers. They are actually sages who after performing austerities for thousands of years have attained perfection. Being *munis*, they are able to discern that you are actually the *ādi-puruṣa*, even though you remain hidden in your form as a young boy at the conjunction of the *paugaṇḍa* and *kaiśora* ages. Therefore they are unable to abandon your company and are following behind you offering prayers."

What is the nature of their prayers? There are so many different kinds of poems and prayers that can be offered to Kṛṣṇa, but amongst them, which are the topmost? There are countless *mantras* within the Vedas, and their personifications pray, "Although we are the *mantras* of the Vedas, up until today we have been performing austerities for the purpose of attaining and becoming absorbed in the *bhāva* that You share with the *gopīs*. Please be kind and make that *bhāva* arise within our hearts." There are so many types of prayers one can offer to Kṛṣṇa, but if someone prays for the *bhāva* of Vraja, then He is more pleased. And especially if someone prays for the *bhāva* of the *gopīs*, that will please Him the most.

Grandfather Bhīṣma prayed, "O Lord, out of friendship You are driving the chariot of Arjuna, and Your blood is flowing from the wounds made by my arrows. At this time I remember You in Vṛndāvana as Your soft body may have been pricked by thorns, and blood is coming from those wounds. Seeing You in this condition, that *bhāva* is coming to me." In Vraja, Kṛṣṇa's skin may have been pricked as He was playing with the *sakhās*, but really Bhīṣma is remembering Kṛṣṇa with His skin having been scratched by the *gopīs* in their amorous pastimes. In describing that *bhāva*, Sanātana Gosvāmī has quoted this verse of Bhīṣma here in his commentary and given a very beautiful explanation. This kind of prayer is the topmost. If we pray, "O Lord, Yaśodā has scolded You and You are crying. I offer *praṇāma* to You in this condition time and again," then Kṛṣṇa will be pleased. But above that, if we pray, "O Lord, You are very *rasika*. In Vṛndāvana, when the *gopīs* are fatigued, You massage their feet and appease them. I offer *praṇāma* to You time and again," then there will be no need to say anything more. Being very pleased, Kṛṣṇa will give Himself to someone who offers such a prayer. He is more pleased by those who pray with this elevated *bhāva* than He was even by the prayers of Brahmā.

The descriptions of Kṛṣṇa's pastimes are referred to here as *akhila-loka-tīrtham* – they are the saviour and purifier of the entire world. One may be purified by repeatedly bathing in holy places, but hearing *hari-kathā* from an elevated devotee will purify one for all time, and make one qualified to purify others as well. Acting as *guru*, this *līlā-kathā* is the purifier of everyone, whether they are qualified or not by other considerations. It is the bestower of the knowledge of Bhagavān's glories, and the very thing that takes us across the ocean of material existence. Singing about Bhagavān's pastimes will purify oneself and the entire world also.

Holy places become very contaminated and even begin to desire that sinful people will not bathe in their waters, but if someone hears *hari-kathā* from Nārada, will Nārada ever become contaminated? Whoever asks him questions and whoever hears his answers will become purified. He is always singing the glories of Bhagavān's pastimes, and sometimes even creates some pastimes himself, such as when he went to Dvārakā accompanied by Uddhava and the construction of Nava-vṛndāvana was arranged. He inspires many different kinds of pastimes, and then he sings about them. No one knows the glories of *līlā-kathā* better than Nārada. If anyone hears and chants such descriptions, especially the descriptions of *līlā* found in *Śrīmad-Bhāgavatam*, then certainly Kṛṣṇa, accompanied by His associates, will appear in that person's heart.

Chapter Six

The Gopīs Desire to Become Birds and Deer

After telling the story of *Śrī Bṛhad-bhāgavatāmṛta*, Sanātana Gosvāmī is giving us some *rasāyana*, some nectar-tonic that is especially for those who have been freed from the disease, but who are still a little weak. By taking this medicine for some time, the body will again become strong, meaning that one will be able to progress in *sādhana* and one's *prema-bhakti* will become steadfast. First he treated our disease, but just curing the disease is not everything because one still remains weak. After one's faith (*śraddhā*) has increased and transformed into resolute determination (*niṣṭhā*), progressing from there he will face many, many impediments to spiritual advancement (*anarthas*). This nectar-tonic is especially intended for those at this stage. If in a regulated manner one hears these final verses and then deeply meditates on them, his love for Bhagavān will surely increase. But if after hearing these verses one doesn't meditate on them, then at the time of chanting the holy name his mind will certainly be absorbed in thoughts of material enjoyment. While chanting his mind will be unsteady, and remembrance of events from the life he led before he began to follow the path of *bhakti* will awaken inside him. Various kinds of *saṅkalpa* and *vikalpa*, attraction and repulsion to material objects, will come to his mind, and he won't receive the full benefit from this nectar-tonic. But if someone meditates on these verses while chanting the holy name, then his *bhakti* will surely increase. *This* is the method for increasing one's devotion.

While we are dreaming, those things which occupied our minds and which we meditated on time and again while awake come to our vision. Sometimes things that are completely unrelated appear in our dream; it is all scrambled and there is not even any realistic continuity. If our minds are not controlled, then it will be the same when we chant *harināma*. For a certain amount of time each day we all hear some *hari-kathā,* but now consider what you are doing for all your remaining waking hours. If we fully meditate on Bhagavān during those remaining hours, then at all times the mind will remain absorbed in Him.

The focus of our minds will be determined by what we think about during our waking hours. If for those hours the mind is pondering over sense enjoyment, such as what arrangements we have made for eating and drinking and how we will solve all of our worldly problems – then how will we be able to steadily think of Bhagavān? Will our minds remain steady while chanting from our daily hearing of perhaps only one hour of *hari-kathā*? It will certainly be absorbed in what we have thought about during most of our waking hours, and even while sleeping we will remember those same things. But if one remains in *sādhu-saṅga* and during all his waking hours applies his mind to hearing *hari-kathā*, reading the scriptures, serving the Lord, and doesn't worry about any other problems, then his mind will remain steady. Therefore the *sādhaka* who wants to elevate his mind should meditate on the pastimes described in these verses while chanting the holy name. We should make this effort, pushing away the thoughts of experiencing sense enjoyment and collecting good quality possessions, and gradually, in due course, our minds will remain steady in meditation on Bhagavān's pastimes.

For this purpose the pastimes of Śrī Caitanya Mahāprabhu are supremely merciful and generous. When Mahāprabhu was in South India, He met with Rāya Rāmānanda, and their conversation, the *Rāmānanda-saṁvāda*, is unanimously appreciated by all the topmost devotees in this world. If you read it you will see why. There, with each verse they are unveiling the deepest of secrets, and while reading it, your heart will become so spellbound that you won't want to put it down. Therefore while chanting *harināma*, we should meditate on these types of narrations from the scriptures. But if we are inattentive while taking *harināma*, we will not be benefited. We should first try to attain *niṣṭhā,* and then *ruci* (taste) will come. After that *āsakti* (deep attachment) will come, and we should try to transform that into *bhāva* (ecstatic emotion). In the *līlā-kathā* that we are hearing here from Sanātana Gosvāmī, there are instructions for all levels of devotees. Those on the level of *śraddhā* will understand these verses in a particular way, and those who have *niṣṭhā* will understand them in a different way. Those in *āsakti* will understand them in a certain way, and those who are in *bhāva* will understand them in yet another way.

Speaking amongst themselves, the *gopīs* said that when all the plants, creepers and trees of Vṛndāvana were trembling in the breeze, it was as if they were experiencing ecstatic symptoms, and that they were drooping down solely to offer their everything to Kṛṣṇa as He passed by. A *sādhaka* should also try to offer his everything to Kṛṣṇa, and when he does, then it can be said that he is really engaged in *sādhana*. Then the *gopīs* remembered how the bees would sit on Kṛṣṇa's garland of forest flowers and not leave Him, and how they would sometimes swarm around Him offering prayers.

Next the *gopīs* describe how the birds are even more elevated, and how they reacted to the sweet melody emanating from Kṛṣṇa's flute. There are birds such as peacocks, parrots, pigeons and koels that live on land, but first they describe the birds that reside on water:

sarasi sārasa-haṁsa-vihaṅgāś
cāru-gīta-hṛta-cetasa etya
harim upāsata te yata-cittā
hanta mīlita-dṛśo dhṛta-maunāḥ

Śrīmad-Bhāgavatam (10.35.11); *Bṛhad-bhāgavatāmṛta* (2.7.114)

[The *gopīs* said:] It is very astonishing that Kṛṣṇa steals away the hearts of the swans, cranes and other water-birds in such a way that they approach Him, sit down and worship Him with their eyes closed, and fully concentrate their minds on Him.

In this verse from the *Yugala-gīta*, the *gopīs* are saying, "Forget those bees; more intelligent than them are these birds who reside on the water." When Kṛṣṇa arrived in the forest, what astonishing thing happened? *Hanta* means "amazed", and being wonderstruck the *gopīs* are now marvelling at seeing these birds. "When the cranes and swans on the pond heard the beautiful song Kṛṣṇa was playing on His flute, they became completely spellbound! Through the medium of their ears they held Kṛṣṇa within their hearts. Ordinarily, when they see someone, they immediately flee; but instead they quickly came near to worship Kṛṣṇa." *Upāsata* means worshipping with the mind, body and words all at once. As long as a *jīva* is conditioned, he is not capable of performing real *upāsana*. He can only be endeavouring for *upāsana*, because it means being near Bhagavān, in His personal presence. When we offer *pūjā* to the deity it is called *upāsana*, but is it really *upāsana*? Where is the deity, and where are we? We are conditioned souls, and He is all-pervading, the solidified form of *sac-cid-ānanda*. Therefore we are not able to really be near Him, but when our hearts are pure enough and we attain a spiritual form, then we can go near Him and it can be called *upāsana*. But as long as we are conditioned souls full of *anarthas*, we cannot really offer Him *arcana*.

So from far away these birds approached Kṛṣṇa with *yata-cittāḥ*, their minds fully controlled, but in our present condition our minds are not controlled. In meditation, there are the stages of *yama* (control of the senses), *niyama* (control of the mind), *āsana* (bodily postures), *prāṇāyāma* (breath control), *pratyāhāra* (withdrawal of the mind from sensory perception), *dhāraṇā* (steadying the mind), *dhyāna* (meditation) and finally *samādhi* (trance), and when one has achieved this state, then his meditation can be called real *upāsana*. So when those birds heard Kṛṣṇa playing the flute and saw His exquisite form, they became *yata-cittāḥ* – fully self-controlled. This is one symptom of a *sādhu*, and two more are described in this verse: *mīlita-dṛśaḥ* – they closed their eyes, and *dhṛta-maunāḥ* – they became silent. Ordinarily they were always making their chirping sounds, but instead they became silent.

Speech is the cause of so many faults. If someone speaks in a deceptive or unbeneficial manner, his mind will be contaminated and therefore become restless. But if one's speech is controlled, then he will never offend any Vaiṣṇava. Fighting and quarrelling – uncontrolled speech is the cause of all this. Therefore in the *Upadeśāmṛta* the first of all instructions given to us is *vāco-vegam* – our speech must be controlled. So here it says *dhṛta-maunāḥ* – the tongues of the water-birds, which ordinarily make so many sounds, at once became silent. If someone desires to engage in *bhajana*, then they should practise silence, which means not speaking anything besides *kṛṣṇa-nāma* or *kṛṣṇa-kathā*. Then it will really be *sādhana-bhajana*. And also *mīlita-dṛśaḥ* – those birds closed their eyes. They took a look at Kṛṣṇa and then immediately closed their eyes: what does that mean? Through the medium of their eyes they took Kṛṣṇa into their hearts, and then they had no desire to see any worldly object. And *yata-cittāḥ* – remaining silent with their eyes closed, their minds became fully controlled. From looking here and there and speaking in an unregulated manner, one's mind becomes restless. For this reason Bilvamaṅgala plucked out both of his eyes and became silent except for speaking *kṛṣṇa-kathā*; but without harming our eyes or tongue we should simply control them, and then automatically our mind will become controlled.

Here the *gopīs* are saying, "This is a very astonishing thing! These birds who ordinarily chirp day and night have today become silent, and closing their eyes they have taken Kṛṣṇa into their hearts. Now automatically their minds have become controlled, and they have no remaining desire in this world." If someone desires to engage in *bhajana*, then they must be like this. This instruction is for all levels of devotees, and according to one's level one will be able to do this. Yet in the *Yugala-gīta* we find, "Aho *sakhī*! We are unable to do this! Day and night our minds are restless. We are not able to keep our eyes closed, and we are also constantly conversing; we are unable to remain silent. The swans and cranes can go near to Kṛṣṇa and receive His direct *darśana*, but we cannot get such a good opportunity. They are certainly of a higher class than us." This is the *gopīs' uttama-adhikārī* vision: even though their eyes remain open solely because they are always searching for Kṛṣṇa, and even though they are unable to remain silent solely because they are always speaking about Kṛṣṇa, they are considering everyone else to be more fortunate than themselves, and they are taking instruction from everything and everyone.

Sanātana Gosvāmī also gives another meaning to this verse being discussed. These birds, being attracted by the sound of Kṛṣṇa's flute, came near Him, but then they too could not remain silent. Very softly they chanted, "*Kṛṣṇa, Kṛṣṇa, Kṛṣṇa.*"

And although they closed their eyes, their minds could not be controlled because waves of ecstasy were flowing inside them. When Kṛṣṇa attracted the *gopīs* in the night by playing the flute, they stood before Him silently. Some of them may have even closed their eyes, but does that mean that their minds were peaceful? On the contrary countless varieties of *bhāva* were churning in their hearts! If anyone goes near Kṛṣṇa, will they be able to remain silent? All the time they will be singing either *kṛṣṇa-kathā* or *kṛṣṇa-nāma* – and will they be able to keep their eyes closed? They will be looking here and there to find the place from which the hypnotic flute sound has come. And will their minds remain steady? Their minds will certainly become even more restless in a state of divine ecstasy!

Next comes this verse:

prāyo batāmba vihagā munayo vane 'smin
kṛṣṇekṣitaṁ tad-uditaṁ kala-veṇu-gītam
āruhya ye druma-bhujān rucira-pravālān
śṛṇvanti mīlita-dṛśo vigatānya-vācaḥ

Śrīmad-Bhāgavatam (10.21.14); *Bṛhad-bhāgavatāmṛta* (2.7.115)

O friend, the birds of Vṛndāvana are actually sages. They have taken positions on the branches of trees, which have new and fresh leaves, from where they can easily have *darśana* of Śrī Kṛṣṇa. Sitting there and hearing the sweet vibration of His flute, they close their eyes and become immersed in divine bliss.

Kṛṣṇa and Baladeva were decorated as if they were dancing actors entering an arena to give a performance. They were adorned with forest flowers and jumped about like young deer. This verse says *vigatānya-vācaḥ* – the birds became silent – which corresponds to what was mentioned in the previous verse. Kṛṣṇa played the flute very beautifully, and at once all the peacocks gathered together. They were sitting in the *kadamba* trees at the top of the mountain, but at once they came down to the meadow to be near Kṛṣṇa. Then so many different varieties of birds came near and watched as Kṛṣṇa was playing the flute and the peacocks were dancing. At that time, seeing through the eyes of *bhāva*, the *gopīs* spoke this verse. In great astonishment they said *prāyo batāmba*. The word *amba* generally means "mother", but does that mean they were speaking to Yaśodā? Will all of these sentiments come to them when they are before Mother Yaśodā? No, that *bhāva* would be constrained. The sentiments of *vātsalya* and *mādhurya* are completely opposed to one another, and neither can remain in the other's presence. So here *amba* means they are addressing another *sakhī*. "O *sakhī*, the birds of this forest are actually *munis* because upon hearing the sweet melody Kṛṣṇa is playing on the flute, they have closed their eyes and are simply remaining silent. They have descended to the trees of the meadow and are sitting on the branches in such a way that there is no obstacle to their seeing Kṛṣṇa, and where Kṛṣṇa can also glance at them affectionately."

Druma-bhujān means "the branches of trees", and can also refer to the "tree" of the Vedas. The Vedic tree has thousands of long branches, and seated on certain branches according to their classification are *karmīs*, *jñānīs*, *yogīs* and *tapasvīs*. The vulture is seated where there are no leaves, and the koel is seated where the mango buds are drooping. Eating these soft buds and leaves, it sings, "*ku-hu, ku-hu*". The peacocks mostly sit in the tops of the *kadamba* trees, and they are very beautiful in appearance and very good dancers. Among the Vedic branches are also seated various kinds of *munis*. Seated on one branch is Patañjali Ṛṣi, on another is Jaimini Ṛṣi and on another is Gautama Ṛṣi. But the birds of Vṛndāvana are different from them, and are sitting on which branch of the allegorical Vedic tree? The branch where the fruit that has no pit – the ripened fruit of the Purāṇas and all scriptures – can be found. That ripened fruit is *Śrīmad-Bhāgavatam*, and sitting on this branch they can taste the *Bhāgavatam*, have *darśana* of Kṛṣṇa, and Kṛṣṇa can affectionately glance at them.

So the *gopīs* are saying, "Certain *munis* have become birds in Vṛndāvana, and upon hearing the beautiful melody from Kṛṣṇa's flute, these *munis* have become silent and are sitting quietly with controlled minds. Just see how fortunate they are, and how unfortunate we are. Being birds they can hear the melody of Kṛṣṇa's flute and approach Him and feel so much *ānanda*, but we can't listen to His flute or go near Him. If we could become koels or parrots or any other bird and go to hear Kṛṣṇa playing the flute at Govardhana and see the peacocks dancing, then our lives would be meaningful."

Next is this verse:

dhanyāḥ sma mūḍha-gatayo 'pi hariṇya etā
yā nanda-nandanam upātta-vicitra-veśam
ākarṇya veṇu-raṇitaṁ saha-kṛṣṇa-sārāḥ
pūjāṁ dadhur viracitāṁ praṇayāvalokaiḥ

Śrīmad-Bhāgavatam (10.21.11); *Bṛhad-bhāgavatāmṛta* (2.7.116)

These ignorant deer are also fortunate, because accompanied by their husbands they are standing motionlessly and listening to the vibration of Kṛṣṇa's flute. It is as if they are offering *pūjā* to the gorgeously attired son of Nanda with their loving glances.

The *gopīs'* meditation became diverted, and again their internal vision was directed towards another group of living entities. They classified the bees as more fortunate than themselves, the swans and cranes as superior to the bees, the birds who reside on land as more fortunate than the water-birds, and the deer as superior to the birds. "Most fortunate of all are these deer, because not only have they at once approached Kṛṣṇa, and not only have they received His loving glance with their eager eyes – but in their exchange of glances was the most affection." *Mūḍha-gatayaḥ* – people call deer foolish. Because the deer easily fall into traps, they are considered foolish as a species. With some simple allurement they can be easily captured. We have heard that sometimes hunters have someone play a flute very sweetly, and being attracted the deer come near and fall into a trap. But the *gopīs* say, "We don't consider the deer to be foolish at all! Hearing the sound of Kṛṣṇa's flute and seeing His gorgeous dress, they have approached Him." *Upātta-vicitra-veśam* means Kṛṣṇa is decorated with forest flowers and leaves such as the fragrant mango leaf. He is adorned with red powder in various places and has the designs of spiders drawn on His cheeks, and upon the body of Govardhana He appears more beautiful than millions of ornaments. *Saha-kṛṣṇa-sārāḥ* means the female deer were searching here and there for Kṛṣṇa, and their husbands were following behind them to protect them. *Pūjāṁ dadhur viracitāṁ praṇayāvalokaiḥ* means that they gazed towards Kṛṣṇa's beautiful face with great love, and it was as if they were offering *pūjā* to Him with their sidelong glances. Upon seeing this, and how affectionately Kṛṣṇa also glanced at them – seeing how much mutual love there was between them – the *gopīs* said, "They have received such a wonderful opportunity, but where is such an opportunity for us? Can we approach Kṛṣṇa and offer *arcana* to Him with our eyes? We are not so fortunate. If after leaving these bodies we could become female deer, then we could receive such an opportunity and our lives would be meaningful."

Chapter Seven

The Animals of Vraja are Stunned

gāvaś ca kṛṣṇa-mukha-nirgata-veṇu-gīta-
pīyūṣam uttabhita-karṇa-puṭaiḥ pibantyaḥ
śāvāḥ snuta-stana-payaḥ-kavalāḥ sma tasthur
govindam ātmani dṛśāśru-kalāḥ spṛśantyaḥ

Śrīmad-Bhāgavatam (10.21.13); *Bṛhad-bhāgavatāmṛta* (2.7.117)

In order to drink the nectarean vibration of the flute-song emanating from the lotus mouth of Śrī Kṛṣṇa, the cows have raised their ears. The grass that they were chewing just remains in their mouths, and milk begins to drip from their udders. The calves at once stop drinking their mothers' milk, and as they embrace Kṛṣṇa within their hearts, tears of love begin to glide down their faces.

The *gopīs* are conversing about Kṛṣṇa in their homes during the daytime. But we are different; upon awakening in the morning we just begin thinking about how to solve all of our worldly problems. Except for a very few persons, no one has the faith or the free time to chant the holy name, and even if someone has some faith and time, then we don't chant in the way we should. *Sādhakas* should learn from the lives of the *gopīs*, who upon awakening in the morning begin meditating on Kṛṣṇa, which means that they begin burning in separation from Kṛṣṇa. Then they bathe and decorate themselves – for whom? Only for Kṛṣṇa. The theme of their conversation is: "How can we meet Kṛṣṇa?

How can we serve Him?" Then they go to Nandagrāma to receive His *darśana* and to cook for Him. When Kṛṣṇa goes to the forest for the day, they return to their homes and converse about Him for the remainder of the day. In each group one *gopī* will be speaking, and so many other *gopīs* will be listening, and there are thousands of these groups. According to their particular natures, they are seated in groups and are singing about Kṛṣṇa's pastimes.

We take our beads and sit to chant, but our minds wander here and there. Then another devotee comes and sits near us, and we begin conversing with him about this or that. We abandon our chanting of *harināma*, and he leaves it also. But the *gopīs* aren't like this; one *gopī* says to another, "Aho! From the lotus mouth of Kṛṣṇa the sound of the flute has emerged. It has crossed the entire *brahmāṇḍa*, crossed Siddhaloka, Vaikuṇṭha, Ayodhyā, Mathurā and Dvārakā, and has now entered Vṛndāvana. While grazing, the cows hear this hypnotic vibration and at once raise their ears. The melody of Kṛṣṇa's flute is like celestial nectar, and it is as if they are drinking that nectar through their ears. And the grass that they had taken in their mouths moments before is just remaining there! They aren't swallowing it, and it isn't coming back out of their mouths either. They are just standing motionlessly and listening.

"And when the calves who are drinking their mother's milk hear the sound of Kṛṣṇa's flute, the milk that they had drawn out remains in their mouths! Usually it is swallowed immediately, but at that time it just remains in their mouths and then gradually begins to glide down from the corners of their mouths. What to speak of just these cows and calves, all the inhabitants of Vraja have become absorbed in the melody of Kṛṣṇa's flute. But we are not so fortunate. These cows and calves are also shedding tears of *prema*, and sometimes even the clouds shed tears of *prema* for Kṛṣṇa as well. But it is our great misfortune that we are so hard-hearted that we don't leave our homes at once and go to where Kṛṣṇa is playing His flute and become equally spellbound. Because we are afraid of being disgraced in society we are holding our patience and not going there, considering that there are too many obstacles. But if someday the sound of the flute really enters our hearts, then at once our patience will fly away and we will immediately run to Kṛṣṇa. If we could give up these bodies right now and take birth as calves, that would be very good! Then whenever we would hear the sound of Kṛṣṇa's flute, we would go there at once! We would be entirely under His protection, and while gazing at Him we would forget everything else."

In this way the *gopīs* are speaking. Just see the nature of their condition, their feelings. For receiving *darśana* of Kṛṣṇa and for hearing the melody of His flute, a *sādhaka* should have such feelings of separation (*vipralambha-bhāva*) in his heart, and then he will be engaging in real *bhajana*. If one's *sādhana* is established on sound knowledge of Vaiṣṇava philosophy and he becomes free from *anarthas* such as fruitive acitivity, cultivating impersonal knowledge, laziness, criticising other devotees and committing offences, then Bhagavān will not be far away from him. Bhagavān is always just behind us, not far away. Paramātmā and *ātmā* are always together; they are not separate. Kṛṣṇa and our very souls are together within us, but at present we are not seeing Him because we don't have sufficient faith.

If a person is crying out from afar, is there any friend or relative who won't come to his aid? Even if there is a son who has given his mother great difficulty, even to the point of trying to kill her, when he calls out in pain, will his mother not come to his aid? Are there any parents anywhere who could possibly ignore the pleas of their offspring? Perhaps only if they don't hear them – but Kṛṣṇa is always nearby, and if we call out to Him, will He not hear? He is much more merciful than mere worldly parents. There is no place where He is not; He is always very near us inside our hearts. If we call Him sincerely, is it possible that He won't hear us? Will Kṛṣṇa not hear if we loudly call out to Him? At present we don't have sufficient faith, but when we pray from deep within our heart with great faith and tears falling from our eyes, "O master of the *gopīs*, please hear my desperate prayer!" will He not hear it? Certainly He will; otherwise His name would have to be changed. When we have this mood, then what we are engaged in can really be called *bhajana*.

Next comes this verse:

vṛndaśo vraja-vṛṣā mṛga-gāvo
veṇu-vādya-hṛta-cetasa ārāt
danta-daṣṭa-kavalā dhṛta-karṇā
nidritā likhita-citram ivāsan

Śrīmad-Bhāgavatam (10.35.5); *Bṛhad-bhāgavatāmṛta* (2.7.118)

Hearing the vibration of Śrī Kṛṣṇa's flute, the bulls, cows and deer of Vṛndāvana approach Him. Unable to swallow the grass that they had taken into their mouths, they stand silently with their ears raised and appear like animals in a painting.

The previous verse is from the *Veṇu-gīta*, and this verse is from the *Yugala-gīta*. "O *sakhī*, hearing the sound of Kṛṣṇa's flute and seeing His attractive form, the cows, bulls and deer of Vraja have become stunned and forgotten everything. They have abruptly stopped grazing and the grass that they were chewing merely remains within their mouths. They have lifted up their tails and raised their ears, trying to discern from which direction that sound has come. When they realise the direction from which it has come, they slowly proceed until they come near to Kṛṣṇa. It is as if the vibration of the flute has entered through their ears, stolen their hearts and again exited their bodies. Therefore what can they do? They must follow that sound until they are near

Kṛṣṇa, and since their hearts are no longer within them, they appear like motionless animals in a painting. Kṛṣṇa's flute-song has stolen their hearts, and feeling themselves possessionless, they have approached Him as if begging alms."

Dhṛta-karṇāḥ – these animals' ears generally droop down, but upon hearing the music of Kṛṣṇa's flute, they raised them. At first they were listening, but then they reflexively turned their ears away from that sound so that it couldn't enter. Why? They were thinking, "We won't allow this sound to enter into our hearts, because then it will steal our hearts and may even steal away our very lives! We may die, and therefore we won't allow this vibration to enter!" Kṛṣṇa's appearance and the vibration of His flute are like nectar and poison simultaneously – *viṣāmṛta ekatra-milana*. It cannot be discerned whether *kṛṣṇa-prema* is nectar or poison, just as when ice is placed in our hand, it feels as if it is burning. We can't tell if our hand is burning or freezing. Similarly, coming in contact with *kṛṣṇa-prema*, we can't discern whether we are feeling ecstasy or sadness. Saccharin has a bitter taste, but if you mix it with water it becomes sweet. And if you suck on a gooseberry, at first it seems sour, but when you get the juice it becomes sweet. Like this, externally *kṛṣṇa-prema* appears to be full of great sadness, and sometimes internally it may even feel something like sadness, but it is really the greatest happiness.

So these cows closed their ears, and when upon opening them a little the vibration of the flute entered, they felt concerned for their very lives. They didn't know whether to accept or reject it. In the same way, some people say, "My friend, there is no need for all of this devotion to God. Those who have *bhakti* actually have no happiness. Even in the stage of *sādhana* they are crying. They think, 'By leaving home to engage in *bhajana*, I have made all of my family members cry, and I am no longer able to live with them.' And look at what the composers of the scriptures have written:

nayanaṁ galad-aśru-dhārayā
vadanaṁ gadgada-ruddhayā girā
pulakair nicitaṁ vapuḥ kadā
tava nāma-grahaṇe bhaviṣyati

Śikṣāṣṭaka (6)

O Lord, when will my eyes be filled with a stream of tears? When will my voice choke up? And when will the hairs of my body stand erect in ecstacy as I chant Your holy name?

"They are praying for the day when they will never stop crying, and they desire to be always wailing in *kṛṣṇa-prema*. Actually it is not really such a surprising thing that they desire to cry in the stage of *sādhana*, because without a child crying, his mother will not feed him milk. All right, so they are crying in the stage of *sādhana* – but just look, then, at their stage of perfection! Uddhava and Akrūra were perfected souls, and we have heard that when they saw Kṛṣṇa's footprints on the ground, they began wailing and even fell down and began writhing on the ground! And until the *gopīs* met Kṛṣṇa again at Kurukṣetra, they were always crying. And when they again parted, they cried even more! Even though they were perfected souls! Therefore all of this *bhakti* is just an unnecessary commotion."

But to persons who say this we say *yayātmā suprasīdati* (*Śrīmad-Bhāgavatam* (1.2.6)): *bhakti* completely satisfies the soul with spiritual bliss. Without engaging in *bhajana*, no one can be happy. Churning water will never produce ghee. Even if all the people of the universe say that churning water produces ghee, will it happen? Never. And without engaging in *hari-bhajana*, no one can attain happiness or cross over this ocean of material existence. This point cannot be refuted any more than the fact that the sun will definitely set in the west. This is confirmed in the

Vedas, the *Rāmāyaṇa* and all of the Purāṇas, and it cannot be refuted.

Meeting with Kṛṣṇa and separation from Him are simultaneously like nectar and poison, and their characteristics cannot be distinguished from one another. They become one and the same thing. Therefore these animals of Vraja become bewildered and concerned for their very lives, while at the same time the *gopīs* are saying, "In Vraja we are the most unfortunate. Everyone else is becoming filled with bliss by receiving Kṛṣṇa's *darśana*, but we must remain here in our homes."

Chapter Eight

The Gopīs Glorify the Pulinda Girl

During the daytime, the *gopīs* are sitting together in their homes and revealing their inner sentiments to one another. One says, "After leaving this body, I desire to take birth as a deer, and then easily I will receive the *darśana* of Kṛṣṇa." Another says, "I desire to become a cow or a calf. Who stops *them* from approaching Kṛṣṇa? Hearing the vibration of Kṛṣṇa's flute, I will approach Him and become spellbound, just as the cows and calves do. In an unrestricted fashion I will receive His *darśana*." In this way some *gopīs* desire to become clouds, and others desire to become bees, birds or rivers. Now, in this verse from the end of the *Veṇu-gīta*, they will begin to speak about those in human form:

pūrṇāḥ pulindya urugāya-padābja-rāga-
śrī-kuṅkumena dayitā-stana-maṇḍitena
tad-darśana-smara-rujas tṛṇa-rūṣitena
limpantya ānana-kuceṣu jahus tad-ādhim

Śrīmad-Bhāgavatam (10.21.17); *Bṛhad-bhāgavatāmṛta* (2.7.119)

O *sakhī*, we consider the Pulinda girls who collect grass and wood to be greatly fortunate, because by spreading the *kuṅkuma* which lies upon the grass on their faces and bodies, the desires which arise in their hearts from seeing that very *kuṅkuma* are pacified. In reality, that *kuṅkuma* is from the breasts of Śrīmatī Rādhikā, and at the time of enjoying pastimes with Śrī Kṛṣṇa, it becomes smeared on His lotus feet. Then as They wander in the forest, it falls from His feet onto the grass.

In previous times in Vraja there was a tribe called Pulinda, who would construct small huts that they would live in for only a short time and then move on. Their women would collect wood or dry plants and sell them to maintain themselves, or they would bring water for people. They were also artists, so they would travel to peoples' homes selling their craftwork. The *gopīs* are saying, "Aho! All of the living entities we have described so far are certainly fortunate, but this girl of the Pulinda tribe is *pūrṇāḥ* – completely fortunate. Why? In the morning, arriving in the valleys of Govardhana to collect wood, she notices that *kuṅkuma* is mixed with the dew on the grass. Seeing this, desire begins to burn in her heart."

Intense eagerness to meet Kṛṣṇa arose in her heart because remembrance of a previous incident came to her. The day before, in a *kuñja* of Govardhana, Kṛṣṇa and His friends were playing dice with the *gopīs*. There were two parties: Kṛṣṇa's party and Śrīmatī Rādhikā's party, and the main players were Kṛṣṇa and Śrīmatī. Subala and Madhumaṅgala and others were on Kṛṣṇa's side, and Lalitā, Viśākhā and the other *sakhīs* were on Rādhikā's side. Kṛṣṇa put up something as a bet and was defeated. Then Rādhikā said, "What will You bet now? You should stake Your flute."

Kṛṣṇa replied, "I will stake My flute, but what will You put up? You should stake an equally valuable thing. I value My flute like My very life, but I will stake it if You stake something of equal value."

Rādhikā said, "Then You please say what I should stake."

Kṛṣṇa said, "All right – You should stake one of the friends of Your *sakhīs*."

Being very pleased, Rādhikā agreed to this and whispered to

one of Her *sakhīs*, "In the village nearby is a girl of the Pulinda tribe. Go and call her." They brought the girl there, and entering that assembly the poor girl felt very shy. She felt ashamed because she was of a lower class, so reluctantly she sat in the back. Seeing her, Kṛṣṇa said, "I will not stake My flute for her! What is the meaning of this?" Then all of the *gopīs* began laughing and clapping. At that time, this Pulinda girl saw the beauty of Kṛṣṇa. Before it was described how all of the birds and animals became spellbound by seeing Kṛṣṇa, but this girl considered herself a maidservant of Rādhikā, so upon seeing Kṛṣṇa she became even more spellbound.

So the next morning while this aborigine girl was collecting wood and plants, she saw *kuṅkuma* lying on the grass, and automatically she knew where it had come from – the breasts of Rādhā. Are the birds, deer or aborigines of Vṛndāvana ordinary? For instance, how do they know Kṛṣṇa is coming in their direction when He is taking the cows out for grazing? They all recognise His intoxicating fragrance. It is expected that the *gopīs* would naturally recognise this fragrance, but even the birds and animals are familiar with it. When the Pulinda girl saw this *kuṅkuma*, such intense desire to meet Kṛṣṇa arose in her heart that she was unable to restrain it.

When Kṛṣṇa is departing Nanda-bhavana to take the cows out to graze in the forest for the day, all of the men, women and children of Vraja assemble along the road to catch a glimpse of Him. They are all standing along the path, and Kṛṣṇa is coming on His way playing the flute. At that time there are also some young girls who come to see Him who are in *śānta-rati*. There are many types of *śānta-rati*, such as *samanya* (general) and *svaccha* (undeveloped). The aborigine girl was *svaccha*, which means that *rati* had arisen inside her, but not *sthāyi-rati*, her permanent internal sentiment. After a seed is planted, a creeper begins to grow from it. At that time its leaves have begun to appear but have not completely developed, and from looking at the leaves you cannot ascertain what kind of plant it is. But when the leaves become full, then you can tell what kind of plant it is. It is the same with *rati*, and the Pulinda girl's *rati* is described as being *svaccha*. Whenever she sees Kṛṣṇa reciprocating with His devotees in a particular mellow, she desires to share that same mellow with Him.

For instance, when she sees Mother Yaśodā nurturing Kṛṣṇa, reciting *mantras* so that no harm will come to Him and wiping His face with the end of her *sārī*, she becomes spellbound. Without blinking she just gazes at Him, thinking, "I would like to be His mother just like her." This is *svaccha-rati*. Then a little later she sees Kṛṣṇa playing His flute, and running, playing and eating with His friends with great pleasure, and then she again becomes spellbound, thinking, "I would like to become a *sakhā* so I can run and play with Him like this." Then later she sees Kṛṣṇa standing in His threefold-bending posture, playing the flute and gazing at the *gopīs*. He is shivering, His crown is tilting to one side and His yellow shawl is slipping down. Seeing this, she thinks, "I would like to become a friend of Rādhā and serve Him with a similar sentiment." This is called *svaccha-rati*.

So this Pulinda girl, in comparison to the creepers, bees, clouds and deer, is the best of all. As a result of witnessing Kṛṣṇa performing His pastimes, and especially from seeing Kṛṣṇa just the day before, she has gradually come to desire to enter the camp of Rādhā's servitors to be able to serve Him as they do. Therefore when she saw the *kuṅkuma* on top of the grass, *smara-rujaḥ* – intense desire to meet Kṛṣṇa arose in her. If eagerness to meet Kṛṣṇa arises even in the birds and animals, then it is even more natural that it would arise in her. If such eagerness develops within a *sādhaka*, then it can be said that he is really engaged in *sādhana-bhajana*. But presently we have no such eagerness to meet Him; instead we are greatly determined to obtain material enjoyment. As yet we have no real eagerness for *bhakti*, but we should endeavour to obtain this eagerness because it is the root, the very life of *bhajana*.

The Pulinda girl looked at the *kuṅkuma* and began analysing it: "Where has this *kuṅkuma* come from? Has it come from the feet of Kṛṣṇa, or the feet of the *gopīs*? *Kuṅkuma* is not applied to Kṛṣṇa; only the *gopīs* apply *kuṅkuma* to their bodies, so how could it have turned up here? This is difficult to understand. Somehow I know that it could have only come from Kṛṣṇa's feet, but how did it get on Kṛṣṇa's feet? Oh, I understand! Fearing that Kṛṣṇa's feet would be harmed by pebbles and thorns as He roams about, the *gopīs* sometimes place His feet on their breasts. Therefore this *kuṅkuma* must have come from Kṛṣṇa's feet as He returned home from His rendezvous with the *gopīs*." Understanding the situation, she at once became intoxicated, placed some of this *kuṅkuma* on her head, and by spreading it all over her whole body, her *kāma* was pacified.

The *Bhāgavatam* says that *kāma*, or lust, exists in the heart of the conditioned soul like a disease. This fire of lust burns inside the conditioned soul as he turns away from Bhagavān and casts his vision in the direction of *māyā*. The conditioned soul becomes attracted to the opposite sex, to wealth and to being praised by others. Some leave material life and take up residence in a temple to engage in *bhajana*, and even attain a little taste for chanting the holy name and hearing *hari-kathā*, then fall down and leave. Why? They were attracted to *māyā*, were they not? Certainly they were very attracted; if they had such strong attraction for the Lord, they wouldn't have entered the material world in the first place. The attraction of *māyā* is very, very strong, and in this connection there is the example of Kālā Kṛṣṇadāsa, a boy of sixteen or seventeen years. Nityānanda Prabhu, Rāya Rāmānanda and

Svarūpa Dāmodara each said to Śrī Caitanya Mahāprabhu, "O Lord, please don't go to South India alone. I will accompany You."

Mahāprabhu replied, "If I take any of you, then the others will say, 'You are taking him, but not me?' Then I will be at fault, so I will go alone."

"All right, then we will send someone whom You are not acquainted with: this simple and honest son of a *brāhmaṇa*. Keep him with You, because how Your mind changes we cannot understand. Sometimes You forget everything, even Your bodily needs. You require *kaupīnas* and a waterpot, so who will carry them? Sometimes You throw them somewhere and proceed onward, and sometimes when You are crying out, 'Where is the Lord of My life?' You roll on the ground, and even if Your clothes were to come off, You wouldn't notice! Crying and crying, You just proceed onward. You will need someone to fetch water and beg alms for You, so please take this Kālā Kṛṣṇadāsa."

Mahāprabhu agreed, and Kālā Kṛṣṇadāsa accompanied Him until they reached Kanyākumārī, where there was a group of gypsies called Bhaṭṭathāris who would travel here and there with their bulls, donkeys and belongings. Their business was to lure young boys and girls to join them – how? They would show boys a girl, and girls a boy. Once they had lured someone they would immediately move on, and the people of the village would not know where their son or daughter had gone. In this way they would set traps for innocent boys and girls, and there was a very large group of these gypsies nearby where Mahāprabhu was staying. One day Mahāprabhu went out begging, leaving Kālā Kṛṣṇadāsa sitting underneath a tree. One of these gypsies approached him, and after speaking with him for some time, said, "It is as if you have been my son for a very long time! Look – we will marry you to this girl, and you will live with her very happily. Within our tribe you will become a king." The poor boy was lured, and decided to go with them.

When Mahāprabhu returned and didn't see him, He thought, "Where has that boy gone? Oh, those gypsies must have taken him!" Mahāprabhu entered their party, and locating Kālā Kṛṣṇadāsa, grabbed him by the *śikhā*, saying, "You rascal! You left Me and came *here*?" He had to forcibly drag back Kālā Kṛṣṇadāsa, who didn't even desire to leave there! So just see how, even if one is associating with Bhagavān Himself, *māyā* can attract him. So what to speak of us? This *māyā* is very dangerous, and escaping its many trappings is very difficult. And even if someone can renounce everything – even his wife and family – still he may not be able to leave the desire for prestige (*pratiṣṭhā*). It is as if the desire for it runs in our veins. But if we receive some special mercy from the spiritual master, the Vaiṣṇavas and Bhagavān, then we will be able to abandon that desire; otherwise we won't easily be able to leave it. We should make our own effort to leave it, but we must also receive their mercy, both.

vikrīḍitaṁ vraja-vadhūbhir idaṁ ca viṣṇoḥ
śraddhānvito 'nuśṛṇuyād atha varṇayed yaḥ

Śrīmad-Bhāgavatam (10.33.39)

If one faithfully hears the five chapters of the *Śrīmad-Bhāgavatam* that describe the *rāsa* dance – Kṛṣṇa's transcendental pastimes with the *gopīs* – then the heart disease of lust will be destroyed. But it must be heard with real faith, which is received from the spiritual master and the Vaiṣṇavas. If one enjoys reading novels, and considers these pastimes between Kṛṣṇa and the *gopīs* to be mere fiction, then it will not have the desired effect. Previously there was this lust in the Pulinda girl's heart, but by the mercy of the great *bhāva* of the *gopīs*, who are Kṛṣṇa's *hlādinī-śakti*, all *anarthas* can be destroyed. Therefore that *kuṅkuma* was the *gopīs'*, and having been smeared on Kṛṣṇa's feet, it now lay on the grass invested with some powerful potency (*śakti*). Having come in contact with both the *gopīs* and Kṛṣṇa, it had become so powerful.

How much *śakti* can be in foot-dust? Once Śrī Rāmacandra was walking along in a forest and he came across Gautama Ṛṣi, who had cursed his wife, Ahalyā, to become stone. When Rāma touched that stone with his feet, she immediately assumed her original form as a very beautiful goddess. She circumambulated him, offered him prayers, and then bid him farewell and left with her husband. So this *kuṅkuma* of the *gopīs* mixed with the dust of Kṛṣṇa's feet will have enormous *śakti*. In this Pulinda girl's heart was the disease of lust, but upon touching this *kuṅkuma* her heart was made supremely pure and was invested with *kṛṣṇa-prema*. Her feelings became like those of the *gopīs*, and following them, she began serving Kṛṣṇa. So in this verse the *gopīs* are saying, "For an aborigine girl, she is so fortunate! Even more so than the female deer. What would they understand of this *kuṅkuma*? But she has understood that this *kuṅkuma* is not ordinary; by touching it the amorous pastimes of Śrī Rādhā and Kṛṣṇa arise in one's heart."

If a *sādhaka* applies the *kuṅkuma* of these descriptions to himself through hearing them – even in *ābhāsa*, the semblance of real hearing – then his heart will also be supremely purified, and all his material desires will be destroyed. Here the *gopīs* are actually singing their own glories, but they're not thinking that way. Whose *kuṅkuma* was this? Their own; yet here, by the influence of Yogamāyā, they are forgetting that and singing the glories of the aborigine girl.

A devotee is one who considers himself extremely fallen. If we are thinking, "I am an advanced devotee and better than others; I can attract people by giving various meanings of Sanskrit verses, I possess so much *bhakti* and so many people are showing me respect," then we have not yet become devotees. When even a little *bhakti* has entered someone's heart, then humility will certainly be there. Where there is no humility, we can understand that there is no *bhakti*. He who has become a better devotee is he whose humility has increased. Where humility exists in its full form, there *bhakti* will also be in its full form. And where there is no humility, there will not be even a trace of *bhakti*. More humility is found in a *madhyama-adhikārī* devotee than in a *kaniṣṭha-adhikārī*, and more humility exists in the *uttama-adhikārī* devotee than in the *madhyama-adhikārī*. Then it is found more in the residents of Goloka Vraja than in the general class of *uttama-adhikārīs*, and amongst the Vrajavāsīs more humility can be seen in the *gopīs*, and amongst them the most humility is found in Śrīmatī Rādhikā. She is the pinnacle of humility. In whomever She detects even a trace of *bhakti*, She considers that person worthy of Her reverence. She offers prayers to that person, thinking, "I should try to become like them."

This is the vision of an *uttama* devotee: "Oh, Kaṁsa is so fortunate! In order to kill Kaṁsa, Bhagavān has come in such an attractive form! He won't kill Kaṁsa's soul, but will show him mercy by releasing him from his body. At the same time, He has bestowed on this world pastimes that are full of unlimited purifying potency. If not for Kaṁsa, then Kṛṣṇa would not have appeared, and His glories would not have become known. Only because of fear of Kaṁsa, Kṛṣṇa was taken to Gokula. Then He returned to Mathurā only to kill Kaṁsa, and then He left for Dvārakā because of Kaṁsa. Why? Jarāsandha's daughters were married to Kaṁsa, so when Kaṁsa was killed, they went crying to their father, 'For some reason Kṛṣṇa has killed your son-in-law!' Taking an army, Jarāsandha attacked Kṛṣṇa seventeen times, so Kṛṣṇa thought, 'Every day there is fighting here, so we should go away from here,' and He left for Dvārakā. It was all because of Kaṁsa. Kaṁsa was not an ordinary person, and that is why a *mahā-bhāgavata* Vaiṣṇava like Nārada would regularly go to see him."

A *madhyama-adhikārī* may feel some hatred for Kaṁsa, but an *uttama-adhikārī* won't. In a similar way, the *gopīs* are considering the Pulinda girl to be superior to themselves and are glorifying her: "If we could take birth as a Pulinda girl, then our mother, father and brothers would not restrict us from seeing Kṛṣṇa during the daytime. We could go to the forest every day and collect wood, but because we belong to higher class families, this is not possible for us now." If a *sādhaka* is to enter into *bhakti*, he must have this humility; and when he does, he can really be called a *sādhaka*.

In the verse we are discussing, why does it say *śrī-kuṅkuma*? It can mean that *kuṅkuma* which carries some special splendour, or it can mean reddish, like Kṛṣṇa's lotus feet. Kṛṣṇa is of a dark blue (*śyāma*) complexion, but the palms of His hands and the soles of His feet are a deep reddish colour. This *kuṅkuma* is of the same hue, and when it came in contact with Kṛṣṇa's feet, it assumed some special splendour and also some special *śakti*. If food is prepared for and offered to Kṛṣṇa, His potency enters into it – Kṛṣṇa's full *śakti* is in *mahā-prasāda*. Upon being touched by Kṛṣṇa's mouth it becomes *sac-cid-ānanda*, just like Him. So before the *gopīs* used this *kuṅkuma* it was not *śrī*, but coming in contact with Kṛṣṇa's lotus feet, all the potency and splendour of those lotus feet entered into it, and it became extraordinarily beautiful. And where did that *kuṅkuma* come from originally? *Dayitā-stana-maṇḍitena* – from Rādhikā, and therefore it can also be said that it became *śrī* from Her touch.

By seeing that *kuṅkuma* lying on the grass in the morning, *smara-rujaḥ* – lust arose in the heart of the Pulinda girl. But when she smeared that *kuṅkuma* on her body, did her lust increase or diminish? All the *jīvas* in Vṛndāvana – the insects, birds, animals and people – are always restless to see Kṛṣṇa; and when they see Him, does their eagerness for Him increase – or diminish? It certainly increases, but when they receive Kṛṣṇa's touch, then they may become a little peaceful. Therefore this *śrī-kuṅkuma* is non-different from Kṛṣṇa Himself; upon seeing it, the eagerness of the Pulinda girl increased, but upon spreading it all over her body, she became fully satisfied, and once again peaceful.

In speaking this verse, the *gopīs* considered the Pulinda girl to be *pūrṇāḥ* – to have become completely fulfilled, even more so than the birds and animals of Vraja. She was not as divinely beautiful as the *gopīs* and was unqualified to participate in amorous pastimes with Kṛṣṇa, but in considering her to be more fortunate than themselves, the *gopīs* are exhibiting a symptom of *mādana*, which is the upper stage of *mahābhāva*. This is when they consider an unqualified person, or even an inanimate object, to be superior to themselves, and even give an explanation of why they feel this way. The flute is an inanimate object, but because it always resides at Kṛṣṇa's lips and never becomes separated from Him, and even though it is of male gender, the *gopīs* feel that it is more fortunate than them. Their sentiment towards the flute is that it is like the second wife of Kṛṣṇa.

So here, this feeling from the upper stage of *mahābhāva* has arisen in the *gopīs* towards the Pulinda girl. It is not possible for other devotees to have this high sentiment, and therefore in places like Dvārakā this sentiment isn't known. This beautiful *bhāva* is found only in Vraja. Even though this girl had no relationship with Kṛṣṇa, seeing how she began shivering and tears began flowing from her eyes when she noticed the *kuṅkuma* from Kṛṣṇa's feet that was lying on the grass, the *gopīs* desired to experience her sentiments. Śrīmatī Rādhikā said, "Such a *bhāva* never comes to us!" Here Rādhikā Herself is singing the glories of the Pulinda girl, and She is not considering the actual elevated state of the *vraja-gopīs*. She is not thinking about that. Whose *kuṅkuma* was it in the first place? Hers, but she is considering the aborigine girl to be more fortunate! This is a symptom of *mahābhāva*. "She is so fortunate! If in My next life I could take birth as a girl of the Pulinda tribe, then there would be no one to prohibit Me from seeing Kṛṣṇa, and I would also be able to experience such a beautiful *bhāva*."

Chapter Nine

Kṛṣṇa Enjoys Playing with His Friends

Superior to the Pulinda girl we have been discussing are the *sakhās*, and of them Śukadeva Gosvāmī says:

yadi dūraṁ gataḥ kṛṣṇo
vana-śobhekṣaṇāya tam
ahaṁ pūrvam ahaṁ pūrvam
iti saṁspṛśya remire

Śrīmad-Bhāgavatam (10.12.6); *Bṛhad-bhāgavatāmṛta* (2.7.120)

During the day, while playing and jumping about with His *sakhās*, if Kṛṣṇa, desiring to see the splendour of the forest, would go to a somewhat distant place, then with great speed the *sakhās* would run to Him saying, "I will touch Him first! I will touch Him first!" and in this way they enjoyed life. They would embrace Kṛṣṇa, and Kṛṣṇa would also embrace them. They would refer to one another as "Sakhā, Sakhā!" and they would carry one another on their shoulders. Because they would play with Kṛṣṇa in such an unrestricted fashion, both indoors and outside, these young *gopas* are superior to the Pulinda girl.

In the early morning Kṛṣṇa would still be sleeping, and Subala, Madhumaṅgala and others would come and jump on His bed to awaken Him. Mother Yaśodā would be hesitant to awaken Him, because generally a sleeping child should not be awakened. If He slept too late, then to awaken Him perhaps she would sing a sweet song and gently sprinkle some water on His face. But the *sakhās* would simply jump on Him, and then they would accompany Him to the forest for the day. While eating and drinking, while inside the house or outside, coming and going, they would always accompany Kṛṣṇa. Seeing this, the *gopīs* say, "These *sakhās* are so fortunate! Day and night, anywhere and everywhere, they are always playing with Kṛṣṇa. If we could become *sakhās*, then we would always feel great happiness! We could always be by His side. Sometimes Mother Yaśodā feeds them at the same time she feeds Kṛṣṇa, and then they play together all day long. In this way they are always fully satisfied."

Singing the glories of the youthful cowherds, the *gopīs* became absorbed in *bhāva*. This is the nature of *prema*, and especially the nature of *mahābhāva*. Recognising even a trace of *prema* in others, the *gopīs* consider them to be more fulfilled than they themselves. When Śrī Caitanya Mahāprabhu was in Purī surrounded by His devotees, a dog approached Him. It was making a whining sound, and tears began to fall from its eyes. Mahāprabhu was eating coconut and gave that dog some of His *prasāda*, and when the next day the dog was nowhere to be found, everyone understood that it went to Vaikuṇṭha. So who wouldn't desire to become that dog and be able to approach Mahāprabhu and receive some of His *prasāda*? Then rolling on the ground in ecstasy, relinquishing his material body and becoming an eternal associate of Bhagavān in Vaikuṇṭha – who wouldn't desire such a benediction? Especially those who have *prema* would desire it. Similarly, upon seeing someone receiving the kindness and affection of Kṛṣṇa – whether they are qualified for it or not – Rādhikā becomes intoxicated and thinks, "They are more fortunate than Me; I wish that My fortune could become like theirs."

Accompanied by countless *sakhās*, Kṛṣṇa takes the calves out to graze for the day. When calves become a little bigger they give up drinking the cows' milk, and Kṛṣṇa takes something like 900,000 of these calves out to graze. Meanwhile Śrīdāmā comes, and how many calves does he have? All of his calves join the procession. Then Madhumaṅgala, Subala, Stokakṛṣṇa, Arjuna and countless other *sakhās* with countless calves join them. Amongst this procession there are different parties, like when a *kīrtana* procession is going along. One party holds a banner with the words "Keśavajī Gauḍīya Maṭha", another holds a banner with the name "Rūpa-Sanātana Gauḍīya Maṭha", and another party hold a banner displaying the name of another temple. Similarly, the *sakhās* are going along together, but in separate parties. Sometimes those who desire to separate during the course of the day do so, but at the end of the afternoon when Kṛṣṇa plays the particular melody on His flute that signifies it is time to return, they again come together. Then upon returning, they again go their separate ways when each *sakhā* takes his calves and goes to his own father's house.

While going along together with their millions of calves, the *sakhās* play their flutes and horns, sing and play various games. In this verse it says *remire*, a derivative of the word *ramanā*, which means to enjoy. Enjoying with His friends, Kṛṣṇa enters the forest, where they decorate each other with the many varieties of flowers and leaves as well as peacock feathers. At once Kṛṣṇa is decorated like the king of dancers, and He also decorates the other boys. Then they begin playing; how does it start? Śrīdāmā steals one of Madhumaṅgala's beloved *laḍḍus* and gives it to another boy, and it is passed around so many times that no one knows where it has gone. Madhumaṅgala approaches everyone asking them, "Have you seen my *laḍḍu*?" and if they have it, they keep it hidden. One *gopa* steals another's flute, horn or stick, and when the owner of it pursues him, he throws it away and then another *gopa* picks it up and runs with it. In this way they play in their attractive childhood pastimes (*bāla-līlā*).

The boys are all laughing and Kṛṣṇa smiles, but if Kṛṣṇa doesn't smile, then everything is spoiled. Everything is going on exclusively for Kṛṣṇa's pleasure. At that time, these children have forgotten their homes, families and even their own bodily needs – everything. One boy is playing the flute, another is singing like a bird, another is mimicking a monkey and another is imitating the sound of a frog. For the purpose of increasing their eagerness, sometimes Kṛṣṇa hides, and then the *sakhās* are unable to stay where they are and they begin searching for Him. If one of them catches a glimpse of Him, then at once they all race there. One after the other they embrace Kṛṣṇa, and laughing, Kṛṣṇa embraces them in return.

When Kṛṣṇa would sometimes go to a slightly distant place to see the splendour of the forest, the *sakhās*, upon losing the great ecstasy (*paramānanda*) they experience by playing with Him, become very unhappy. Sanātana Gosvāmī says in his commentary that Kṛṣṇa plays with the *sakhās* for nine hours each day while taking the cows and calves out to graze. So when do the *gopīs* receive the opportunity to be with Him for that long? At that time, by the arrangement of Yogamāyā, Kṛṣṇa assumes two forms. In one form He remains playing with the *gopas*, and in the other form He enjoys with the *gopīs* at Kusuma-sarovara or Rādhā-kuṇḍa. Or on some pretext He tells the *sakhās*, "I am going to Kusuma-sarovara to get a drink of water," and by the influence of Yogamāyā He seems to return in one second only. The *gopas* don't know how much time has elapsed, just as an entire night of Brahmā elapsed while the *rāsa* dance was being performed. During the *rāsa-līlā*, did any of the members of Kṛṣṇa's or the *gopīs'* households know of it? They considered that it was only an ordinary night lasting eight hours. So either by assuming two forms or remaining in only one form, Kṛṣṇa would sometimes also enjoy with the *gopīs* during the day.

Next comes this verse:

ittham satāṁ brahma-sukhānubhūtyā
dāsyaṁ gatānāṁ para-daivatena
māyāśritānāṁ nara-dārakeṇa
sārdhaṁ vijahruḥ kṛta-puṇya-puñjāḥ

Śrīmad-Bhāgavatam (10.12.11); *Bṛhad-bhāgavatāmṛta* (2.7.121)

In this way the greatly fortunate cowherd boys enjoy in various ways with Śrī Kṛṣṇa, who is seen as the Brahman effulgence by the *jñānīs*, as the supremely worshipful deity by His servants and as an ordinary boy by people in general. (Or, the word *māyāśrita* can also mean that those who had received His utmost mercy, due to being devoid of the mood of opulence, saw Him merely as the son of Nanda.)

Kṛṣṇa had killed Aghāsura, and while taking the cows out to graze during the daytime, the *sakhās* were playing with the demon's bones and skin. There was no bad odour coming from the demon's body, and all the *sakhās* thought, "How has it become dried out like this?" Because Kṛṣṇa had assumed the forms of those cowherd boys for one year immediately after the killing of Aghāsura, they thought that only one day had elapsed since the demon was slain. Brahmā had hidden them in a cave for one year under mystic trance, but when Kṛṣṇa glanced at them they revived, and the expanded forms of cowherd boys entered back into His original form. When Kṛṣṇa killed Aghāsura, the effulgence of the demon's soul merged into Kṛṣṇa's feet. Brahmā and many *yogīs* were watching this and thought, "Who is this? He appears to be an ordinary young boy, so how is this possible?"

This verse says *satām,* which means saints who are always fixed in meditation. For them Kṛṣṇa is the personification of the joy derived from immersion in the impersonal Brahman, and for devotees who consider themselves His servants, He is *para-daivatena* – the supreme god. When Kṛṣṇa entered the wrestling arena of Kaṁsa, who saw Him as the *para-devatā*? The Vṛṣṇis, who considered Him to be their worshipful deity, but the *gopīs* and other residents of Vraja didn't see Him like that. Some saw Him as a friend, some as a son and some as a paramour. *Māyāśritānāṁ nara-dārakeṇa* – and those under the influence of *māyā* saw Him as an ordinary young boy. The cowherd boys were playing with Him because *kṛta-puṇya-puñjāḥ* – by their "accumulation of pious activities", they were able to enjoy with Him in this way.

There are three meanings of the word *puṇya*. First it can mean conventional pious activities, but performance of this type of *puṇya* does not qualify one to meet Kṛṣṇa. Secondly it can mean *sukṛti*, and by accumulation of this one receives *sādhu-saṅga*, then they may accept the shelter of a spiritual master, and then develop *bhakti*. And when *bhakti* becomes perfected, *prema* comes, and when one has this *prema*, then he can meet Kṛṣṇa. By the *puṇya* of personalities like Mahārāja Hariścandra, Dadhīci Ṛṣi or Mahārāja Śibi,[3] can one meet Bhagavān? No. By the practice of *sādhana-bhakti* one won't meet Bhagavān, and even by possessing *bhāva-bhakti* one won't meet Him. When one has *prema-bhakti*, then he can meet Kṛṣṇa. Don't consider all types of *bhakti* to be one and the same. The cultivation of *sādhana-bhakti* will gradually elevate one, by *bhāva-bhakti* one *may* receive some *darśana* of Kṛṣṇa, but only *prema-bhakti* can overpower Him. To become

3. The story of Mahārāja Hariścandra is found in *Śrīmad-Bhāgavatam*, Ninth Canto, Chapter 7. A description of Dadhīci Ṛṣi is found in *Śrīmad-Bhāgavatam*, Sixth Canto, Chapters 6–7, and a description of Mahārāja Śibi is found in the purport to *Śrīmad-Bhāgavatam* (1.12.20).

Kṛṣṇa's friend and live with Him may not even be accomplished by having *prema-bhakti* if one does not have the *bhāva* of Vraja. These *sakhās* possessed this *prema-bhakti* with *vraja-bhāva*, and that is the meaning of *kṛta-puṇya-puñjāḥ*.

Sanātana Gosvāmī describes how the *sakhās* would play together with great intimacy. Sometimes they would run and play with Kṛṣṇa without any clothing. They would eat from each other's plates and place food in each other's mouths, and they had no fear of reprimand from their elders or anyone. Speaking this verse, Śukadeva Gosvāmī felt great *ānanda*, though he could not remain solely on this topic for long. He is the parrot of Rādhikā, and there is nothing that can fully immerse him in *ānanda* which doesn't include Her name. But here he became spellbound in *sakhya-rasa*, and that *bhāva* poured forth from his heart in the form of his words. In this verse he has used the word *satām,* which means "saint", and here it refers to those who view Kṛṣṇa as the personification of *brahmānanda*, the bliss derived from immersion in the impersonal Brahman. It refers to those who are adorned with the twenty-six qualities of a devotee and who are *jñāni-bhaktas* like the four Kumāras. But if Rūpa and Sanātana Gosvāmīs had personally described a saint by their *own* definition, they would have referred to those who have the *bhāva* of Vraja, and amongst them those who possess the *bhāva* of the *gopīs*, and out of them the one who possesses the *bhāva* of being a maidservant of Śrīmatī Rādhikā.

Once, Durvāsā Muni came and saw Kṛṣṇa playing with His friends. The boys were putting dust on top of Kṛṣṇa's head, and Kṛṣṇa was chasing them and throwing dust on them also. They were sometimes embracing one another, sometimes singing and sometimes verbally abusing one another as children do. Durvāsā thought, "What is this? He who is the very embodiment of

Brahman has taken birth in the house of Nanda?" Gazing in Kṛṣṇa's direction, he became spellbound and just stood motionlessly. Kṛṣṇa saw him from a distance, and at once left His playing and approached him, saying, "Bābā, I have defeated Subala!" Then Subala came and said, "I have defeated Kanhaiyā!" Another boy came and said, "I defeated Kṛṣṇa!" and then Kṛṣṇa said, "No Bābā, I defeated *him*!" Durvāsā could only silently gaze at Kṛṣṇa, and then he sat down. He couldn't determine who defeated who and was unable to give them a verdict. Then Kṛṣṇa sat in his lap, and grabbing his beard, said, "Bābā, you don't speak? Are you deaf and dumb?" Then, feeling restless, Kṛṣṇa raced away from there smiling, and began playing again.

Durvāsā had not entered Vraja after only one or two days' journey; he had been wandering for millions of years and had seen countless universes, countless Brahmās and Śaṅkaras – and after that he entered Vraja. Wonderstruck, he thought, "Here, playing with these boys, is the personification of *brahmānanda*?" From a distance he offered obeisances so as not to disturb Kṛṣṇa's pastimes, and then he went away from there. This is the vision of Kṛṣṇa being referred to in this verse by the line *itthaṁ satāṁ brahma-sukhānubhūtyā*.

Then the next line refers to devotees who see Kṛṣṇa as *para-devatā*, their supremely worshipful deity. And then the third line says *māyāśritānāṁ nara-dārakeṇa*, which means that those under the influence of *māyā* see Kṛṣṇa as an ordinary child. But one more meaning has been given here: if this were to refer to those souls trapped in material illusion, then the sequence would be inconsistent. First was described how the sages see Kṛṣṇa, and then how the devotees see Him, so here *māyāśritānām* must refer to those who are under the influence of Yogamāyā. Sanātana Gosvāmī quotes this verse:

kātyāyani mahā-māye
mahā-yoginy adhīśvari
nanda-gopa-sutaṁ devi
patiṁ me kuru te namaḥ

Śrīmad-Bhāgavatam (10.22.4)

O Kātyāyanī, O possessor of the Yogamāyā potency, please give us the boon of having Kṛṣṇa as our husband.

So in the verse we are discussing, *nara* means that those who have taken shelter of Yogamāyā saw the son of Nanda Mahārāja as an ordinary boy. They didn't see Him with *aiśvarya-bhāva*, awe and reverence, but with *mādhurya-bhāva*, loving friendship. They always played with Him in *nara-līlā*, His pastimes in human form, never considering Him to be the Supreme Lord. If Kṛṣṇa ever tried to tell them that He was Bhagavān, the *gopīs* would start clapping and say, "What, *You* are Bhagavān? You are only a liar and a cheat, and when You are hungry You break Your mother's pots of yoghurt!" So here, *māyāśritānām* must refer to the *gopīs* who by reciting this *siddha-mantra* and offering *pūjā* to Kātyāyanī received Kṛṣṇa as their paramour. Otherwise the sequence of the verse would be incorrect. And in the words *nara-dārakeṇa*, the word *dāra* can also mean "wife", so in this way it also refers to the *gopīs*, who always saw Kṛṣṇa as an adolescent (*kiśora*), handsomely decorated like a new bridegroom, and appearing supremely attractive as the king of dancers. This verse is saying that with this dearest paramour of the *gopīs*, the *sakhās* are playing all day long, so how fortunate must they be considered to be?

Chapter Ten

The Glories of Sakhya-rasa

yat-pāda-paṁśur bahu-janma-kṛcchrato
dhṛtātmabhir yogibhir apy alābhyaḥ
sa eva yad-dṛg viṣayaḥ svayaṁ sthitaḥ
kiṁ varṇyate diṣṭam aho vrajaukasām

Śrīmad-Bhāgavatam (10.12.12); *Bṛhad-bhāgavatāmṛta* (2.7.122)

Great *yogīs* perform severe austerities for many lifetimes, but even when with great difficulty they have completely controlled their minds, they still cannot attain even one particle of the dust of the lotus feet of Śrī Kṛṣṇa. How then can I possibly describe the good fortune of the Vrajavāsīs, who daily received His direct *darśana*?

Yogīs, through many births of practising *yama*, *niyama*, *āsana*, *prāṇāyāma*, *pratyāhāra*, *dhāraṇā*, *dhyāna* and *samādhi*, are unable to touch even one particle of the dust of Kṛṣṇa's lotus feet. They perform such severe austerities but are unable to reach Him, and this refers to Brahmā also. Brahmā has a very long lifespan, and he even sees Kṛṣṇa sometimes, but when he approached Kṛṣṇa, did he receive the dust of His feet? When Brahmā came to Vṛndāvana, Kṛṣṇa was absorbed in playing with His friends. When Brahmā arrived, Kṛṣṇa glanced at him, but then quickly returned to playing. Brahmā could only offer prayers, and didn't directly receive the dust of His feet. So what to speak of ordinary *yogīs*? But that very Vrajendra-nandana, although He is Bhagavān

Himself, stands before the Vrajavāsīs and even plays with them. Even the children younger than Kṛṣṇa would desire to accompany Him when He took the cows out for grazing; they certainly wouldn't just remain in their homes! The mothers of these children would tell Kṛṣṇa, "Look after my son today," and Kṛṣṇa would take those small boys with Him. What to speak of just playing with them, after walking some distance, Kṛṣṇa would ask one of them, "Are you feeling tired?" and He would lovingly take him on His lap and begin massaging his feet.

In this verse Śukadeva Gosvāmī says, "Aho! While taking the cows out to graze, Kṛṣṇa will sometimes even massage their feet! With His own hands He decorates the youthful cowherd boys, and they also decorate Him! They play games together, and when Kṛṣṇa is victorious He smiles with great joy. They eat together, and play jokes on one another – who can describe the good fortune of the Vrajavāsīs? *Pāda-pamśuḥ*, the dust of Kṛṣṇa's lotus feet, which even the *yogīs* are searching for in their meditation, falls from His feet and is spread all around as He jumps about, as His friends massage His feet and as He climbs the *kadamba* trees. And Yaśodā wipes away the dust from Kṛṣṇa's face and applies fresh *añjana* to His eyes. And as He dances with the *gopīs*, with His own hands He wipes the dust from their lotus faces and places it on His head. Tell me, how glorious is that dust? Who can describe it?"

Quoting these verses in his *Bṛhād-bhāgavatāmṛta*, spiritual ecstasy swells in the heart of Sanātana Gosvāmī, as if he is churning cream and tasting its very essence. Then another feeling comes and he quotes this verse:

kvacit pallava-talpeṣu
niyuddha-śrama-karśitaḥ
vṛkṣa-mūlāśrayaḥ śete
gopotsaṅgopabarhaṇaḥ

Śrīmad-Bhāgavatam (10.15.16); *Bṛhad-bhāgavatāmṛta* (2.7.123)

Becoming fatigued from wrestling and playing, Kṛṣṇa spreads His feet out, and one *sakhā*, his heart melted with love and affection for Him, takes Kṛṣṇa's feet on his lap. Millions of *sakhās* arrange millions of beds made of flowers for His comfort. Then, unknown even to Himself, by Yogamāyā, Kṛṣṇa expands into millions of forms and accepts the service of each and every one of them. Otherwise, if millions of *sakhās* all came at once to massage His feet, there would be competition and a great commotion. Therefore Yogamāyā arranges everything very beautifully so that there will not be any conflict. Underneath the cooling shade of a tree, the *sakhās* use their own laps as pillows for Kṛṣṇa and gently lull Him to sleep.

pāda-saṁvāhanaṁ cakruḥ
kecit tasya mahātmanaḥ
apare hata-pāpmāno
vyajanaiḥ samavījayan

Śrīmad-Bhāgavatam (10.15.17); *Bṛhad-bhāgavatāmṛta* (2.7.124)

At that time, one greatly fortunate *sakhā* would massage His feet, and another would fan His body with a fan made of leaves.

Because they would massage Kṛṣṇa's legs with great love, here the *sakhās* are referred to as *mahātmās*, great souls. There are millions of *sakhās* and all are exalted. Some would fan Him, but not with a *cāmara*; with a fan made of leaves and peacock feathers they would fan Him with great love. They serve Kṛṣṇa by providing their own laps as pillows for His head – can such good fortune be seen anywhere else? Their affection for Kṛṣṇa is supremely natural in the mood of *nara-līlā*, considering Him to be an ordinary child. Seeing how Kṛṣṇa has exerted Himself in wrestling with them and in taking the cows out to graze, the *sakhās* serve Him with great affection to remove His exhaustion. When Kṛṣṇa was driving Arjuna's chariot and the sharp arrows of Bhīṣma were piercing Him, did anyone on the battlefield feel any real pain because of that? But are the *sakhās* like this? To remove even one drop of perspiration from Kṛṣṇa's brow they are prepared to give up their very lives.

Because the *sakhās* are engaged in massaging Kṛṣṇa's legs, they are described as *mahātmās. Mahātmā* means "a great soul", and when does one become a great soul? When he attains the service of Kṛṣṇa – otherwise not. Here the word *mahātmanaḥ* can also be an adjective for Kṛṣṇa, who is full in six opulences and who, though being *ātmārāma* (self-satisfied) and *āptakāma* (without desire), still desires to accept service from others. Because He never really becomes exhausted, He has no need for the beds of flowers arranged by the *sakhās.* If after fighting with so many demons and holding up Govardhana Hill for seven days He did not become exhausted, then how could playing with some small children exhaust Him? Thinking, "They have such sincere desires to serve Me that they have come running to Me?", then – although He is Parabrahma and *āptakāma* – still He melts in emotion and lies down on the beds that they arranged and falls asleep. For this reason He is referred to as a *mahātmā. Mahātmā* can also mean "glories", and Kṛṣṇa's glories are the six opulences that He possesses.

Though it seems that these glories would not be exhibited as He is playing the part of an ordinary young boy in this *nara-līlā*, He manifests these opulences by expanding into millions of forms to accept service from each and every *sakhā*, and not even one *sakhā* knows of it. If Kṛṣṇa were to display to them that "I am the possessor of all opulences and can assume unlimited forms," then becoming astonished, they would all begin offering prayers, and there would be no service for Kṛṣṇa to accept. Therefore He is *mahātmanaḥ*.

It is like when someone gives millions of rupees in charity but doesn't think anything of it. This is the glory of giving charity, but if someone gives something and then says to others, "Do you understand how much I have given?" then it is not glorious. Sudāmā didn't consider what he gave Kṛṣṇa to be important, his wife didn't consider it to be, and no one in the entire world would consider it to be anything substantial; but that offering was the most glorious.[4] In the same way, the *sakhās* are giving their everything, their *prema*, and because by manifesting His opulences Kṛṣṇa gives everyone an opportunity to serve Him, He is *mahātmanaḥ*. In the *rāsa-līlā* He gave all of the *gopīs* an opportunity, and in the pastime of bewildering Lord Brahmā He gave all of the cows and older *gopīs* the chance to become His mother by expanding into so many forms, and in both *līlās* no one knew of it. Therefore in this verse the adjective *mahātmanaḥ* is more appropriate in referring to Kṛṣṇa.

There are countless parties of *sakhās* that all have their respective leaders, and just as there are various kinds of *gopīs*, there are also five kinds of *sakhās*: *sakhā*, *priya-sakhā*, *preṣṭha-sakhā*, *parama-preṣṭha sakhā* and *priya-narma-sakhā*. Amongst them are thousands of parties, but there is never any conflict in their service. When the prime minister comes here, many congressmen say, "I will garland the prime minister!", and there is commotion. But there are millions of *sakhās* and there is never any conflict because Kṛṣṇa's divine power (*aiśvarya*) is wonderful. Each and every *sakhā* thinks, "Today I am the most fortunate; Kṛṣṇa has given

4. This story is found in *Śrīmad-Bhāgavatam*, Tenth Canto, Chapter 81.

this good opportunity to me only because He loves me so much!" Yogamāyā arranges everything so that neither Kṛṣṇa nor the *sakhās* know what is happening, otherwise Kṛṣṇa won't be able to taste the *sakhya-rasa*. But this way He can simply go on playing with the boys and tasting the *rasa*.

In this verse the words *hata-pāpmānaḥ* don't mean "without sin", because there is no possibility of sin in the *sakhās* anyway. It means that they served Kṛṣṇa with melted hearts and great affection. Sometimes we serve with love, but mostly we serve because we feel that it is our duty. But if service is done out of pure affection, then Bhagavān will really desire our service. So *hata-pāpmānaḥ* means that the *sakhās'* service was free from any feelings of duty, and with fans made of leaves and peacock feathers they softly fanned Kṛṣṇa to relieve His exhaustion. But it can also have one more meaning: by hearing descriptions of the lives of great devotees such as these *sakhās*, all of one's sins will be eliminated, and for those whose internal forms are as *sakhās*, intense hankering for this type of service will arise within them.

Seeing all of this in his internal identity as Lavaṅga-mañjarī, Sanātana Gosvāmī is submerged in *sakhya-rasa*, thinking, "I would also like to become a *sakhā* and serve Kṛṣṇa in that intimate way." Then he quotes the next verse:

anye tad-anurūpāṇi
manojñāni mahātmanaḥ
gāyanti sma mahā-rāja
sneha-klinna-dhiyaḥ śanaiḥ

Śrīmad-Bhāgavatam (10.15.18); *Bṛhad-bhāgavatāmṛta* (2.7.125)

My dear Mahārāja, other *sakhās* would sing attractive songs appropriate for resting-time, and all the cowherd boys' hearts would melt in affection for Kṛṣṇa.

Some other boys then began singing charming songs that were tasteful to Kṛṣṇa. They sang songs of Kṛṣṇa's childhood pastimes that were *manojña* – so full of *rasa* that it caused Kṛṣṇa's heart to overflow with blissful feelings. Here the word *mahārāja* refers to Parīkṣit Mahārāja, who being very *rasika* is the cause of Śukadeva Gosvāmī speaking such beautiful things.

If Sanātana Gosvāmī had not come to this world, then such simple, beautiful and sweet explanations of these verses would have never been given. Even Śrīdhara Svāmī, the famous commentator on the *Bhāgavatam*, didn't give explanations like Sanātana Gosvāmī's; his explanations were mostly in relation to *vaidhī-bhakti* and for showing the difference between our philosophy and Advaitavāda. Śrī Caitanya Mahāprabhu respected Śrīdhara Svāmī's commentary, and using that as a foundation, Sanātana Gosvāmī established Mahāprabhu's beautiful transcendental sentiments of *bhakti* in his own commentary on the Tenth Canto. Then Jīva Gosvāmī gave further light to that explanation with his *Laghu-vaiṣṇava-toṣaṇī* commentary, and accepting both of those commentaries as remnants, Viśvanātha Cakravartī Ṭhākura extracted the *rasa* from them and composed his own commentary. Hundreds of commentaries on the *Bhāgavatam* have been written, but none of them are as beautiful as his.

The cowherd boys, their hearts melted in great affection, sang beautiful songs for Kṛṣṇa's pleasure. Seeing that Kṛṣṇa was fatigued, the *sakhās* made pillows of their own laps and placed Kṛṣṇa's head there. Kṛṣṇa never really becomes tired, but seeing their desire to render service He became fatigued. As Kṛṣṇa was lying like this, some were massaging His legs, others were rubbing His back, others were rubbing His head, and by looking at His face it appeared that He was resting comfortably and His fatigue was fading.

Sneha-klinna-dhiyaḥ means that with tears in their eyes and melted hearts, the *gopas* sang softly in such a way as to lull Kṛṣṇa to sleep. They sang songs related exclusively to Kṛṣṇa's boyhood pastimes that would give Kṛṣṇa the most pleasure. Sanātana Gosvāmī says in his commentary that these boys' voices were as beautiful as the birdsong of the koel. After all, they are eternal associates of Kṛṣṇa, so will they be any less expert than Him in singing? Madhumaṅgala and Subala could sing just as sweetly as Kṛṣṇa, just as Mahāprabhu's associates could also sing very sweetly. They sang softly and sweetly to increase Kṛṣṇa's pleasure, and they sang in the melody which was appropriate for the afternoon time.

Once, before Nārada had learned the art of singing, he went to the heavenly planets and began singing. The words of the song were good, but it was out of tune and the melody was not correct. Present there in heaven is the demigod of melody named Sura, and upon hearing Nārada singing out of tune he actually became physically deformed. Everyone there who heard Nārada's singing felt pain in their hearts. Then someone approached him and said, "My friend, your singing has caused Sura and all of the beautiful singers present here to become ugly and deformed, so you should immediately go to Brahmā and learn the art of singing."

So Nārada went to Brahmā, and Brahmā told him, "You should approach Sarasvatī and learn from her." Sarasvatī taught him how to sing the appropriate melodies, and when he returned to the heavenly planets and sang again, all of the residents there were restored to their original forms. Then Nārada became the greatest preacher in the world of beautiful devotional songs. If in *kīrtana* the correct melody is not sung at the appropriate time, then it will be inauspicious. In the morning we sing a particular melody, and in the evening we sing a different one. If we don't sing the appropriate melodies according to the time, then Sura, the demigod of melody, will suffer greatly. Those of us here who have to hear it will feel pain, and he will also feel pain.

Knowing all the appropriate songs and melodies, the *sakhās* were all masters of singing. In the same way, Lalitā, Viśākhā, Tuṅgavidyā and all of the *sakhīs* are also expert in singing as well as in all other arts. The *sakhās* are not less skilful than Kṛṣṇa in singing ability, and they have the skill to slowly raise and again lower their pitch to create very wonderful melodies. This expertise cannot be attained in only one life; if someone has it, then we can understand that it is coming from previous lives.

Kṛṣṇa was resting with His eyes closed, and listening as the *sakhās* did wonderful things with gentle waves of sound. At that time Kṛṣṇa was more grave than millions of oceans, and for His pleasure the *sakhās* softly sang songs which, being saturated with *bhakti*, were very tasteful to Him. They sang songs describing the glories of His playful activities, the glories of Mother Yaśodā and the glories of the *gopīs'* love for Him. In this way, their hearts full of *rasa*, they softly sang to Kṛṣṇa in the afternoon, and listening more and more with feelings of great bliss, Kṛṣṇa closed His eyes and became overwhelmed with *prema*.

When we offer food to Kṛṣṇa, what are our feelings? We chant the *mantra*, but is the necessary *bhāva* there, or not? Our feelings should be like those of Mother Yaśodā: with great affection she seats Kṛṣṇa and pampering Him, begins to feed Him, saying, "Take a little of this, it is very nice... Here, take some of this, it is the nicest." Tell me, then, with how much *prema* is she feeding Him? We should try to offer food to Kṛṣṇa with these feelings, and sing *kīrtana* at that time with the feelings of Bhaktivinoda Ṭhākura. When we make an offering, we sing the songs he has written – "*Bhaja bhakata-vatsala*" and "*Yaśomatī-nandana*" – but generally we only memorise them and don't consider the feelings within them. There are so many beautiful sentiments in those songs, and this is how the *sakhās* serve Kṛṣṇa – massaging Him with great affection, and singing to Him with great *bhāva*. At once their hearts melted, and as Kṛṣṇa was listening, His heart also melted. Therefore Śukadeva Gosvāmī, being very *rasika*, said *sneha-klinna-dhiyaḥ* – Kṛṣṇa was overpowered by *prema* and rendered helpless. Once the singing started, even if someone wanted Kṛṣṇa to get up and move to another place, He couldn't; being spellbound, He could only remain in the same position, with His heart melted and tears rolling down His cheeks. Seeing Kṛṣṇa like this, in this verse Śukadeva Gosvāmī has described Him using the word *mahātmanaḥ*.

Śrīla Sanātana Gosvāmī has given still one more meaning here: *mahātmanaḥ* can also mean *lampaṭa-śekhara*, the king of debauchees. While Kṛṣṇa seems to be asleep, He is listening to the *sakhās* singing songs about His pastimes that are full of His mischievous pranks. Taking the *gopīs'* clothes, He climbed a tree, leaving the poor girls shivering in the water and begging for their clothing back. He said, "You have all committed offences, so you must come before Me and beg forgiveness." In beautiful, soft voices the *gopas* sang songs of pastimes like this and Kṛṣṇa's blissful feelings at once increased.

Kṛṣṇa is supremely *rasika*, and He is *sarvajña*, the knower of all. But still, even though He knows what they will sing next before they actually sing it, when He hears it He becomes overwhelmed with *prema* and tears begin to flow from His eyes. And He receives much more pleasure from their singing than He does from their massaging Him. Their singing is what really makes Him rest comfortably – and from this we can understand that *kīrtana* is the best service. Although all the cowherd boys were massaging Him and this certainly increased His *prema*, when their service included *kīrtana*, which is *bhagavat-priya*, the service most dear to Kṛṣṇa, just see how wonderful His condition became! His *prema* increased until He was completely overwhelmed.

In this verse the word *mahārāja* appears. What is its meaning? *Mahān rūpeṇa rājate* – he who is radiant with some special splendour. He in whose mind the desire for worldly enjoyment doesn't shine, but instead whose thinking is always resplendent with thoughts of *bhagavad-bhakti*, is called "Mahārāja". Here it can refer to Parīkṣit Mahārāja, and it can also mean that these most charming pastimes of Kṛṣṇa with the *sakhās* are the *mahārāja*, or best of all *līlās*. If one hears and chants the descriptions of these pastimes where Kṛṣṇa is playing in His full glory with the *sakhās*, then he also becomes fully glorious and can also be called Mahārāja.

Hearing Śukadeva Gosvāmī describe how the *sakhās* relaxed Kṛṣṇa, how Kṛṣṇa's heart was at once melted in affection, and how He became so overpowered that He was unable to even move, Parīkṣit Mahārāja said, "Aho! Who can conceive of their good fortune?" This description influenced him so deeply that tears began to glide down his cheeks, and his heart also melted. *This* is why in this verse Śukadeva Gosvāmī refers to him as Mahārāja: in its full form *bhakti* had entered his heart, and *prema* began to flow there. Seeing that he was fully qualified to hear the transcendental glories of the fortunate cowherd boys, Śukadeva Gosvāmī referred to him as "Mahārāja".

The word *mahārāja* can also refer to those pastimes that are the best of all. Through their singing, the *gopas* are bringing remembrance of the *gopīs* to Kṛṣṇa. Being very pleased, Kṛṣṇa smiles from ear to ear, and then the *sakhās* also begin to smile, thinking, "He is appreciating what we are singing." *Mahārāja* can also be an adjective to describe the cowherd boys, whose hearts are always saturated with simple, natural *sakhya-bhāva*. Being overwhelmed in their intimate service to Kṛṣṇa, they would experience *anurāga*, and sometimes even *mahābhāva*. In her *vātsalya*, Mother Yaśodā may sometimes experience *anurāga*, but she never experiences *mahābhāva*. But sometimes it comes to Madhumaṅgala, Subala, Śrīdāmā, Arjuna and other *priya-narma-sakhās*. Their pristine hearts radiant with the wealth of *rasa*, they softly sing songs that increase the blissful ecstasy of both Kṛṣṇa and themselves.

Chapter Eleven

Nanda and Yaśodā's Love for Kṛṣṇa

Next, in Sanātana Gosvāmī's heart, feelings of *vātsalya-bhāva* begin to come, and he begins quoting verses describing that sentiment:

nandaḥ kim akarod brāhman
śreya eva mahodayam
yaśodā vā mahā-bhāgā
papau yasyāḥ stanaṁ hariḥ

Śrīmad-Bhāgavatam (10.8.46); *Bṛhad-bhāgavatāmṛta* (2.7.126)

[Śrī Parīkṣit Mahārāja asked:] My dear *brāhmaṇa*, which supremely auspicious *sādhana* did Nanda perform, and which austerities did the supremely fortunate Yaśodā undergo to have her breast-milk drunk by Śrī Hari?

Once, after Kṛṣṇa had eaten some soil, Mother Yaśodā forced Him to open His mouth, and when He did, she saw the entire creation therein. Seeing so many universes with so many Śivas and Viṣṇus, she thought, "What is this?" When Kṛṣṇa revealed His universal form (*viśva-rūpa*) to Arjuna, Arjuna thought "He is Bhagavān!" and with folded hands began offering prayers, but Yaśodā didn't do this. Trembling, she thought, "Has a ghost possessed me? Has someone cast a spell on my child? Is this the illusory energy of the demigods, or what? What has happened to my child?" Rubbing her eyes in astonishment, she looked again and then it had all disappeared. She thought, "Whose illusory energy was this? How did it happen?" She didn't consider that "He is the Supreme Lord!" She continued to see Him only as a small child.

Being very frightened, she took Kṛṣṇa to the family priest and told him, "I saw something very astonishing within my child's mouth. Someone must have cast a spell upon Him! Please rid Him of this curse." The family priest said, "Don't be afraid, we will immediately make Him all right. You bring some gold, some cloth and some cow dung, and bring some cows to give in charity to the *brāhmaṇas*." After she had brought all of these things, the priest chanted the appropriate *mantras* and Mother Yaśodā's mind was set at ease.

In this verse Parīkṣit Mahārāja says, "Considering Kṛṣṇa to be his son, Nanda Bābā loves Him so much; he takes Kṛṣṇa on his shoulders saying, 'My dear son, my dear son!' and for this reason he is *mahodaya*. But greater than him is Mother Yaśodā, who is *mahā-bhāgā* – the most fortunate! Although Hari steals away the hearts of everyone in the entire universe and is the nurturer of all, she takes Him on her lap and feeds Him breast-milk! What auspicious activities did they perform in their previous lives to receive such benedictions?"

Now Sanātana Gosvāmī will begin describing the good fortune of Yaśodā and Nanda Bābā so that their mood of service will begin to arise within us. By hearing the descriptions of these pastimes, all the contamination within one's heart will be eradicated, and feelings of spontaneous love for Kṛṣṇa will be permanently established there. If we hear these types of descriptions during the day and then meditate on them during the night, then that is called *smaraṇa*, and from that eventually *samādhi* will come, so is there any greater *sādhana* than this? When he was hearing the *Bhāgavatam* from Śukadeva Gosvāmī, Parīkṣit Mahārāja only continued listening and hardly spoke at all. Therefore this *sādhana* is also *sādhya*, the final result. By hearing *hari-kathā* one's heart will be completely purified, whereas by practising any other limb of *vaidhī-bhakti* it won't happen as quickly.

The Universal Form is an aspect of the Supreme Lord's great divine opulence (*aiśvarya*), but upon seeing it, not even a trace of *aiśvarya-bhāva* arose in Yaśodā. Instead her *prema* for Kṛṣṇa only increased, and continuing to see Him merely as a small child, she bathed Him in cow dung and cow urine for auspiciousness. Bhagavān is the personification of auspiciousness, yet to bring auspiciousness to Him, she sang some *mantras* and gave charity to the *brāhmaṇas*! Sanātana Gosvāmī says here in his commentary that if one hears these descriptions of Yaśodā endeavouring to bring auspiciousness to Kṛṣṇa, then very soon that same auspiciousness will come to that person. And if a *sādhaka* hears these descriptions with love and deeply meditates on them, then his tendencies towards *aiśvarya-bhāva* will be blocked and he will be able to feel pure *vātsalya-bhāva*. Therefore any trace of *aiśvarya-bhāva* was covered by Yogamāyā, and Yaśodā was able to taste *mādhurya-bhāva* (where a devotee never considers Kṛṣṇa to be Bhagavān Himself, but merely their dear friend, son or lover). Being wonderstruck, Parīkṣit Mahārāja is saying, "Aho! Yaśodā possesses even more good fortune than Nanda! Nanda is certainly fortunate – that is true; but Yaśodā is even more so because she was actually able to bind Kṛṣṇa, whereas Nanda could only later untie Him."

In this verse Parīkṣit Mahārāja addresses Śukadeva Gosvāmī as *brāhmaṇa*, and Sanātana Gosvāmī says in his commentary that Śukadeva Gosvāmī is the direct embodiment of Parabrahma. Generally a devotee is not referred to in this way, but he has done it because here *brahma* means he who is speaking such a high level of *hari-kathā* that it increases the *prema* in others. The *jīva* is part and parcel of Parabrahma, but when he takes shelter of

Parabrahma, then he experiences *prema* as a part of the whole. Because Śukadeva Gosvāmī increases that *prema*, he has been referred to here as the direct embodiment of Parabrahma.

Parīkṣit Mahārāja is asking, "Which auspicious activities did Nanda and Yaśodā perform to receive Kṛṣṇa as their son?" What activities did Prahlāda Mahārāja perform to receive such *bhakti* for Bhagavān? By unknowingly fasting and staying awake all night on Nṛsiṁha-caturdaśī, in his next life, while remaining in his mother's womb, he heard the science of the Supreme Lord from Nārada for sixty thousand years, and after taking birth he became the great devotee Prahlāda Mahārāja. By keeping company with the spiritual master and the Vaiṣṇavas one becomes like that. For us also: if we observe Janmāṣṭamī, Gaura-pūrṇimā or Nṛsiṁha-caturdaśī by fasting and hearing *hari-kathā* all day and serving the spiritual master and the Vaiṣṇavas with great enthusiasm and love – even if it is not for sixty thousand years or even sixty years, but only for sixty months or even sixty days – then that is *sādhana*.

In the lives of all great devotees such as Rūpa and Sanātana this enthusiastic spirit can be seen. But being wonderstruck and feeling that it is impossible to perform such activities in this world that would bestow upon one the benediction of having Kṛṣṇa as their son, Parīkṣit Mahārāja is asking this question. He was completely astonished at the elevated *vātsalya-prema* that Yaśodā and Nanda possessed for Kṛṣṇa. Bhagavān has had many parents, but neither Vasudeva and Devakī, nor Daśaratha and Kauśalyā, nor Kaśyapa and Aditi possessed such a beautiful sentiment towards Him as did Yaśodā and Nanda. Vasudeva and Devakī were unable to taste the *rasa* of Kṛṣṇa's pastimes; immediately after Kṛṣṇa's birth Vasudeva took Him to Gokula, and there His pastimes began. On the first morning, Yaśodā was awakened by the sound of Kṛṣṇa crying, and then an immensely blissful festival was held. The news of Kṛṣṇa's birth spread in all directions, and people came from all over to see Him. The residents of Gokula tasted the *rasa* of Kṛṣṇa's childhood pastimes, but Vasudeva and Devakī were unable to taste even a little of it.

In their previous lives, Nanda was the Vasu demigod Droṇa and Yaśodā was his wife Dharā, and for the purpose of obtaining a very beautiful son they performed very severe austerities. After some time, Brahmā appeared before them and said, "You may ask any boon from me." They said, "Just as parents love a son, we want to have love like that towards Bhagavān." Brahmā said, "So it shall be." Sanātana Gosvāmī also says that Vasudeva and Devakī in their previous lives were Kaśyapa and Aditi, and they performed austerities until Bhagavān Himself appeared before them and said, "What do you desire?" They replied, "We desire a son like You." Bhagavān said, "There *is* no one like Me, so I Myself will become your son."

Bhagavān gave that boon Himself, and before this Brahmā had given that boon. But if Brahmā did not have *vātsalya-prema* himself, then how could he possibly give it? The answer is that Bhagavān protects the words of His devotees, but also, because Brahmā knows past, present and future, he knew that Bhagavān would soon be taking birth in Gokula and performing childhood pastimes, so he gave his boon to Droṇa and Dharā, and Bhagavān fulfilled his words and later came as their son.

Were Droṇa and Dharā ordinary *jīvas*? No, they were plenary portions of Nanda and Yaśodā who, for the purpose of showing the people of this world what type of *sādhana* is necessary to completely overpower Bhagavān, performed severe austerities to receive the boon of having Bhagavān as their son. Both Bhagavān and His devotees can give boons, but the devotee's boon will certainly be more powerful and more filled with *rasa*. Therefore Bhagavān fulfilled the boon given to Droṇa and Dharā, and in their next lives they appeared in their original forms as Nanda and Yaśodā and received Kṛṣṇa as their son.

In comparison to the boons given by Bhagavān Himself, the boon given by the devotee will be superior and bestow a higher taste. If Rāmacandra has taken a vow and Hanumān has also taken a vow, then if their vows conflict, whose vow will be triumphant? Once, seeing the offences of some man, Rāmacandra told him, "Tomorrow morning I shall come and certainly kill you." So who could possibly save him? There was no one who could save him. Later that day, as Nārada was walking along, he came across this man, and seeing his face, said, "My friend, what is wrong? Why does your face appear withered in despair?"

The man said, "Rāmacandra has vowed that tomorrow He will certainly kill me." Grasping Nārada's feet, he cried, "O my Lord, please protect me!"

Nārada said, "Me? I am not able to save you, but you can do one thing: go and grasp the feet of Hanumān, and don't let go! Don't tell him the reason you have grasped his feet, but just beg him to make a vow to always protect you. Then afterwards you may reveal to him the specific nature of your dilemma."

So this man approached Hanumān, and falling on the ground, grasped his feet and cried out, "O Prabhu! Please protect me, please protect me!"

Hanumān said, "Hey! What do you want? Let go of my feet!"

"No Prabhu, I will never let go! Only when you vow to always protect me will I let go!"

"All right, all right, I will always protect you, so what is it?"

"Rāmacandra has vowed that before the sun rises tomorrow morning He will certainly kill me."

"Oh, I see! So who told you to do this? You must have met some intelligent man… or do you have a *guru*?"

"It was Nārada."

This is Nārada's nature, sometimes creating a quarrel between Bhagavān and His servants. So when the morning came, Hanumān told the man, "Just stand behind me, and everything will be all right." Seeing that Rāma was coming, Hanumān picked up His club and assumed a fighting posture. Fixing an arrow to His bow, Rāma said, "Now I will kill this offender."

Hanumān replied, "My Lord, if You desire to kill him, it will only be over my dead body! I have vowed to always protect him." Then Rāma retracted His vow, and honoured the vow of Hanumān. Amongst all of His qualities, Bhagavān's special affection for His devotees is the supreme quality. Therefore He fulfilled the boon that Brahmā had given to Droṇa and Dharā.

We are more interested in taking shelter of Bhagavān's topmost loving (*parama-premī*) devotees. It is a special characteristic of those of us in the Gauḍīya *sampradāya* that we don't actually take shelter of Kṛṣṇa. Even though He is the one who possesses all *śakti*, who is the unlimited ocean of *rasa*, who is supremely merciful, who is especially affectionate to His devotees, who is beginningless and who is the cause of all causes, who is it that we take shelter of? Śrīmatī Rādhikā – and if we don't directly take shelter of Her, then we take shelter of Lalitā or Viśākhā and aspire to become the *dāsī* of the *dāsī* of the *dāsī* of Rādhikā. We should always consider ourselves to be the devotee of the devotee of the devotee, and then Kṛṣṇa will be more pleased with us. He has said, "One who says that he is My devotee is not really My devotee. But he who says that he is the devotee of My devotee is more dear to Me."

Next comes this verse:

tato bhaktir bhagavati
putrī-bhūte janārdane
dampatyor nitarām āsīd
gopa-gopīṣu bhārata

Śrīmad-Bhāgavatam (10.8.51); *Bṛhad-bhāgavatāmṛta* (2.7.127)

[Śrī Śukadeva Gosvāmī replied:] O Bharata, for fulfilling the promise of His dear devotee Brahmā, Śrī Kṛṣṇa, the Supreme Lord Himself and the destroyer of evil, appeared as the son of Nanda and Yaśodā. In comparison to all of the other *gopas* and *gopīs*, this couple possessed the most love for Him.

In this verse Śukadeva Gosvāmī addresses Parīkṣit Mahārāja as *bhārata*. The ordinary meaning is that Parīkṣit Mahārāja was the leader of his dynasty after the great war at Kurukṣetra, but the word *bhārata* can also be interpreted like this: *bhā* can mean *bhavati*, and *rata* can mean *rati*. So since the actual meaning is he who has special *rati* or *prema* for the feet of Bhagavān, just see the respect Śukadeva Gosvāmī is giving him! This verse says that in Vraja there were a great many couples of *gopas* and *gopīs* who had offspring, and all of these couples had *vātsalya-prema* for Kṛṣṇa. Desiring to taste their parental love, Kṛṣṇa expanded into the cowherd boys and became their son for one year during which time He tasted that *vātsalya-rasa*, and so also did all of the parents as they nurtured Him. But amongst all of these couples, Yaśodā and Nanda still had stronger feelings of *vātsalya* for Him than anyone. The other couples loved Kṛṣṇa even more than their own sons, and only when He expanded into their sons during the pastime of bewildering Lord Brahmā did they show equal affection to their own sons.

He also expanded into the calves so that the cows could taste *vātsalya-rasa*, and of course He was also the son of Devakī and Vasudeva. But as described in the previous verse, no one experienced the ecstasy which Yaśodā did as Kṛṣṇa drank from her breasts. Devakī could have only experienced this for a few seconds, because immediately after Kṛṣṇa took birth He was taken to Gokula. At that time milk came to her breasts, and Kṛṣṇa was a small baby of a suitable age to drink her milk, but He was taken away. When Kṛṣṇa first appeared to them in the jail, with folded hands they had offered prayers; but later, when Kṛṣṇa returned to Mathurā and freed them, Kṛṣṇa covered their *aiśvarya-bhāva* by His Yogamāyā. He sat on Devakī's lap and cried "Mother, Mother!", but at that time she could not feed Him breast milk. Eleven years had elapsed, and the opportunity to breast-feed Kṛṣṇa had long passed.

So this verse says that this *dampatī*, this couple Yaśodā and Nanda, were superior to all the other couples of *gopas* and *gopīs* in Vraja. They experienced innumerable wonderful sentiments of parental love, but very few of them have actually been described in *Śrīmad-Bhāgavatam*. The pastime where Dāmodara was bound by Yaśodā is described, and it also describes the time when Kṛṣṇa was very small He got up from Yaśodā's lap and began to crawl towards the door. But hearing some jingling sound, He turned around wondering where that sound was coming from, and was astonished to find that it was the jingling of His own ankle-bells. Then at once Yaśodā caught Him and placed Him back on her lap. Devakī never experienced any of this, and no other *gopī* in Vraja ever experienced so many feelings of *vātsalya*. The *Bhāgavatam* has described only a few of these pastimes, but Yaśodā felt countless millions of wonderful sentiments, such as when Kṛṣṇa played and when He drank her breast-milk. And to understand her elevated sentiments for Kṛṣṇa is very difficult.

When Uddhava visited Vṛndāvana, he saw Nanda and Yaśodā. Nanda was weeping bitterly, and Uddhava could not understand why he was crying. Even right up until the very end of his stay in Vraja he did not fully understand why Nanda was crying so bitterly. Uddhava thought, "Kṛṣṇa is Parabrahma, He cannot really be anyone's son! So towards Him, Nanda has such feelings? Is this some kind of illusion, or what? I know full well that Kṛṣṇa is Bhagavān, so how can I be attached to the idea that He is my friend?" Uddhava could only feel *aiśvarya-bhāva* towards Bhagavān, so seeing this *bhāva* in Nanda Bābā, he couldn't understand it. This is how he felt coming before the great mountain of Nanda Bābā's *mādhurya-bhāva*. When we look at a one-storey building, our head can be held level looking straight ahead. But when we look up at a seven-storey building, then we must tilt our head back slightly. And when we look up at a high mountain, we must tilt our heads back to the point where if we are wearing a hat, it will fall off. So looking up at the towering mountain of Nanda Bābā's *mādhurya-bhāva*, it was as if Uddhava's hat of *aiśvarya-bhāva* fell off! Being so intelligent, a scholar and a disciple of Bṛhaspati, still Uddhava couldn't understand, "Why is he crying like this? This is certainly a matter of great good fortune, that Kṛṣṇa has appeared in his home! Okay, so Kṛṣṇa told me that I should give His parents some consolation. But what will I say? Will I say, 'Nanda Bābā, you are so fortunate! If there is any person in this entire universe who is fortunate, it is you! Please cry more and more! It is said that if even one tear is shed for Bhagavān, then one's life has become completely successful!' Devotees pray for the day when upon hearing descriptions of Bhagavān's pastimes, taking His name, and seeing the places where He has performed His pastimes, they will shed tears and their voices will become so choked that they won't even be able to pronounce His name properly! And here I see Nanda Bābā crying, and how is he crying? Very bitterly, like he will never stop!"

It is said that if someone sheds a tear out of love for Bhagavān, then their life will automatically become successful and they will become the purifier of the three worlds. In one place Uddhava has said:

vande nanda-vraja-strīṇāṁ
pāda-reṇum abhīkṣṇaśaḥ
yāsāṁ hari-kathodgītaṁ
punāti bhuvana-trayam

Śrīmad-Bhāgavatam (10.47.63)

I repeatedly offer my respects to the dust from the feet of the women of Nanda Mahārāja's cowherd village. When they loudly sing the glories of Śrī Kṛṣṇa, the vibration purifies the three worlds.

Why does their *kathā* purify the three worlds? The tearful, deeply emotional songs which they sang to one another became verses in the Tenth Canto of *Śrīmad-Bhāgavatam*, and the scriptures say that when one attains the *darśana* of such a great personality who is crying in this way, one's life becomes successful. But do we ever cry while describing Kṛṣṇa's pastimes or while chanting His name? So tell me, then – how fortunate is Nanda Bābā to be crying, considering Kṛṣṇa to be his son?

So Uddhava was thinking, "Will I say, 'Nanda Mahārāja, you are most fortunate, so please cry more and more because by receiving your *darśana* today my life has become successful'? That will be like adding ghee to the fire! But if I say, 'Nanda Mahārāja, please don't cry, be peaceful', then that will be opposed to what is said in the scriptures." This was Uddhava's curious predicament, and it was as if he were trapped. "If I tell him not to cry, it will be opposed to the words of the scriptures and I will be punished, and if I tell him to cry more, I will not be consoling him as Kṛṣṇa asked me to. Should I tell him to stop crying, or to cry even more?" He was unable to reach a decision, so in the end he mixed them both by saying, "Nanda Mahārāja, you are the most fortunate person, but please don't cry." In this way he was perplexed because Kṛṣṇa had instructed him to console His parents.

Sitting nearby was another fortunate soul, Yaśodā. Her tears had long dried up; the poor woman could not even shed tears. Her eyes were sunken in and she appeared like a skeleton. In one sense she died on the day Akrūra took Kṛṣṇa to Mathurā, and later she sent a message to Kṛṣṇa, "I don't even have the qualification to call You 'my son'. Now, having gone to Mathurā, You have accepted Devakī as Your mother and Vasudeva Mahārāja as Your father. For eleven years here, You were our very lives. As Your *dhātrī* – the one who raised You – I held You in my lap and protected You, and did everything one could expect from a *dhātrī*. Koels lay their eggs in the nest of a crow, and then the crow sits on the eggs until they hatch. When they have hatched, then the mother koel returns and takes the chicks to her own nest and raises them there, and the crow just remains gazing in their direction. Our situation is exactly like that."

Then Kṛṣṇa sent this message back to Yaśodā with Uddhava: "Because you have used the word *dhātrī* to describe yourself, Baladeva and I should give up our lives at once! I am sustaining My life solely to see you again; otherwise I would die today. We will certainly be returning to you soon, because besides you we don't know any other mother. Therefore, Mother, please do one thing: Father will be crying, the cows and calves will be crying, the plants which I planted will be drying up, and the calves which we used to take out to graze will no longer be taken out and will begin dying. Please look after them a little; they will even give up eating out of separation from Me." Seeing and hearing all of this, Uddhava was wonderstruck. Yaśodā was unable to speak; she could only softly stammer. The affection of Yaśodā for Kṛṣṇa, her *vātsalya-prema*, was unlimited, like a fathomless ocean. Uddhava was not able to give her any consolation. Our *gosvāmīs* have not described much of this *vātsalya-bhāva*, because there are very few who are actually qualified to hear it. Therefore they have kept it hidden.

The word *janārdane* comes in this verse, and two meanings have been given for it. The one who destroys whatever is opposed to devotion and establishes *bhakti* is called Janārdana, and *ardana* can also mean a prayer. Therefore it can refer to Droṇa and Dharā, who prayed to Brahmā for receiving that Janārdana as their son, whose prayers were completely fulfilled, and who tasted the highest degree of *vātsalya-bhāva.* Nanda and Yaśodā's *bhāva* is higher than the *vātsalya-bhāva* of all the other *gopas* and *gopīs* in Vraja, and this is the purport of this verse.

Chapter Twelve

Mother Yaśodā's Bhakti is Indescribable

Droṇa and Dharā's receiving Brahmā's boon of having parental love for Kṛṣṇa is similar to Kṛṣṇa's receiving the boon from Lord Śiva of having Sāmba as His son. At that time in Dvārakā, Kṛṣṇa performed austerities for instructing people that by worshipping Śiva, material wealth can be obtained. In reality no one can be Kṛṣṇa's son – Pradyumna, Aniruddha, Sāmba – they are all Bhagavān's plenary portions, but they appeared in the forms of His sons. Yaśodā and Nanda Bābā are the eternal parents of Kṛṣṇa, but for showing that some austerities are necessary to attain love for Kṛṣṇa, the boon was given to Droṇa and Dharā. All of the Vaikuṇṭha incarnations are plenary portions of Nārāyaṇa, and in a similar way, Droṇa and Dharā, Vasudeva and Devakī, Daśaratha and Kauśalyā, and Kaśyapa and Aditi are all expansions of Nanda and Yaśodā. Still, amongst all of the eternal associates of Bhagavān, the eternal associates of Kṛṣṇa are the best.

nandaḥ sva-putram ādāya
proṣyāgatam udāra-dhīḥ
mūrdhny avaghrāya paramaṁ
mudaṁ lebhe kurūdvaha

Śrīmad-Bhāgavatam (10.6.43); *Bṛhad-bhāgavatāmṛta* (2.7.128)

When magnanimous Nanda returned from Mathurā, he took his own son Śrī Kṛṣṇa on his lap and experienced immense pleasure by repeatedly smelling His head.

Previously Nanda Bābā was very detached from worldly life, but after Kṛṣṇa was "born", he became spellbound in attachment for Him. Before Kṛṣṇa's birth, Nanda Bābā never had any need to go to Kaṁsa's kingdom. But after His birth some money was necessary for His sustenance, and for this reason Nanda went to Mathurā. There he spoke to Vasudeva, who told him, "Please, you must return to Gokula quickly! The demons will now create a disturbance in all directions! Kaṁsa is determined to see that all children born within the last ten days are killed. Therefore please return quickly!" As Nanda was returning to Gokula, he saw the massive corpse of Pūtanā beside the road, and being frightened for Kṛṣṇa's welfare, he hurried home.

Arriving there and seeing that Kṛṣṇa was all right, it was as if his very life had returned to his body. His previous feelings of detachment could not remain. Taking Kṛṣṇa on his lap, magnanimous Nanda Mahārāja time and again smelled his son's head, saying, "Bhagavān has saved You from great danger!" Then he heard from his brother Upananda and others how the *rākṣasī* Pūtanā took Kṛṣṇa on her lap and forcibly put her breast in His mouth. She had applied poison to her breast, so how could Kṛṣṇa possibly have been saved? Next she flew up into the sky because Kṛṣṇa had latched onto her and would not let go, and she was thinking that if she could fly to where Kaṁsa was, Kaṁsa could separate Kṛṣṇa from her. She thought that in one minute only she could arrive there, but instead Kṛṣṇa sucked her breast with such force that He not only drank her poisoned breast-milk, but sucked out her very life. Hearing how Kṛṣṇa was saved from the hands of death, Nanda's tears soaked Kṛṣṇa's body.

In this verse are the words *sva-putra*, which mean that Kṛṣṇa was Nanda's own son, and also the word *proṣyāgata*, which means that Nanda was not the actual father of Kṛṣṇa, but the one who nurtured Him. Most people consider that Nanda Mahārāja was Kṛṣṇa's *proṣyāgata*, and that His real parents were Vasudeva and Devakī. Vasudeva brought Kṛṣṇa to Gokula, and there Nanda raised Him. But Nanda Bābā trusted what he saw with his own eyes – that Kṛṣṇa had taken birth from the womb of Yaśodā in his own home. There was no doubt in his mind, but Vasudeva also had no doubt that Kṛṣṇa was *his* son. But if Kṛṣṇa had taken birth in Nanda's home, then how could He have had loving affairs with the girls there, who are the daughters of Nanda's brothers, and therefore would have been Kṛṣṇa's cousins? How would this be possible? The *gopīs* are actually His *hlādinī-śakti*, but He first appeared in Mathurā to prevent the people of this world from saying, "Oh, He is performing the *rāsa* dance with His own cousins!" So it is said that Kṛṣṇa is really the son of Vasudeva, but this verse refers to Kṛṣṇa as Nanda's *sva-putra*, his own son. What could be greater evidence than this? *Nandaḥ sva-putram ādāya proṣyāgata udāra-dhīḥ* – with natural, simple-hearted feelings of great fatherly affection, Nanda took his own son on his lap and nurtured Him. Here, the meaning of *proṣyāgata* is "nurtured".

After the killing of Kaṁsa, Nanda remained waiting in his Mathurā residence and was feeling very unhappy. He was thinking, "More than twenty-four hours have passed since Kaṁsa was killed, and still neither Vasudeva nor anyone else such as Ugrasena or Akrūra has brought me any news. Kṛṣṇa and Balarāma themselves have also not come; because they are mere children that is alright, but why haven't any of the others come? I have heard that people are saying that they are actually the sons of Vasudeva." Because no one went to him with any news, Nanda Bābā was crying in solitude, thinking, "What will I do? Should

I go to Vasudeva's palace to meet him, or what should I do?" Soon after dark, Kṛṣṇa and Baladeva came alone to him. They saw that their father was very sad, with his head hanging down in his hands. Sitting on his lap and lifting up his father's chin, Kṛṣṇa said, "Father, why are you sitting like this, alone and silent?"

Looking at Baladeva, Nanda said, "My son, why haven't you come earlier?"

Baladeva replied, "Father, a very strange thing is happening! Many people are saying that we are actually the sons of Vasudeva, but I don't accept this. Even if we are the sons of Vasudeva, we don't know any other father besides you! If for any reason a mother and father renounce a son, then those who raise him are really his mother and father. There are many different kinds of fathers: the one who begets you, the one who raises you, the king, the spiritual master, the father-in-law and the family priest. But amongst them, the best is he who raises and protects you, and therefore I am your son only, and I don't know any other father besides you. I don't want to remain here in Mathurā for even one more second; I want to immediately accompany you and Kṛṣṇa back to Vraja!"

Nanda Bābā said, "My son, don't speak like this! Hearing this, my younger brother Vasudeva will die, and Devakī will also die!" Nanda Bābā said this because he knew that they really would die, and therefore he is more magnanimous than Vasudeva and Devakī, who didn't care as much about the Vrajavāsīs' feelings while Kṛṣṇa stayed with them in Mathurā. He said to Baladeva, "Six of their sons were killed, and only with great difficulty were they able to save both of you. If you hadn't been brought to Gokula, you would have also been slain. Therefore we are forever indebted to Vasudeva, so you remain here! I will take Kṛṣṇa and return to Gokula."

Baladeva replied, "I will not be without Kṛṣṇa for even one

second! I consider you to be my only father, and Kṛṣṇa to be my only brother!"

Then Nanda Bābā looked at Kṛṣṇa, because in His childhood Kṛṣṇa had given Nanda so much good advice. He asked Him, "What should I do?"

Kṛṣṇa replied, "Father, may I speak?"

"Yes, please."

"In My opinion it would not be auspicious for Baladeva Prabhu to go to Vraja, leaving Vasudeva and Mother Devakī in such a difficult situation. And if I go, then he must go also. Therefore if you will give us permission, we will stay here for a few days, and then later we will both return together." What He was saying was having some influence on Nanda Bābā, but Nanda could only remain silent. Kṛṣṇa continued, "I am prepared to go with you now, but then everyone will say, 'Nanda Bābā is very cruel! Even after all of Vasudeva and Devakī's children died, he took both Kṛṣṇa and Balarāma away from them and returned to Gokula, leaving them to die also!' So please don't do this. Kaṁsa has now been killed, and we just need a few more days to complete our work here by killing all the remaining demons. You please return home."

Concerning this point, Śrīla Viśvanātha Cakravartī Ṭhākura says that a person will stay with whomever he receives the most affection from, whoever they are. Each and every *jīva*, even a dog, is hungry for love. It is true that Kṛṣṇa could not receive the *prema* of Vraja anywhere else. He was not able to obtain even a fraction of the love that Yaśodā and Nanda had given Him in either Mathurā or Dvārakā, and the *prema* that the *gopīs* had for Him was so pure that He could not find anything like it anywhere else in the entire universe. So giving up that love, He went to Mathurā? Viśvanātha Cakravartī Ṭhākura says, "We don't have any faith in that. People may say that He left Vraja and went to Mathurā, but that can't be so! He remained in Vraja in an unmanifest form. No one could see Him, but He was there.

"When Akrūra took Kṛṣṇa and Baladeva on the oxcart to Mathurā, it was actually their expansions in the mode of *aiśvarya* as the sons of Devakī and Rohiṇī that went to Mathurā. They remained in Vraja in their original forms, but no one knew of it. How was this possible? By the Yogamāyā potency, which makes the impossible possible." Therefore Kṛṣṇa always remains in Vṛndāvana; this is the special conception given by our *gosvāmīs*. If Kṛṣṇa was ever able to actually leave Vraja, then it would mean that the residents there didn't love Him the most and that Kṛṣṇa didn't love them the most, and neither of these ideas are possible. Therefore He never leaves Vṛndāvana.

What happened next? Kṛṣṇa began living in Mathurā, and all of the members of the Yadu dynasty returned. Due to fear of Kaṁsa's atrocities they had fled, but after Kaṁsa's death they returned to Mathurā and began living there again with great happiness. Meanwhile, Astī and Prāptī, the daughters of Jarāsandha who had married Kaṁsa, approached their father bewailing, "Your son-in-law was faultless! They threw him on the ground and killed him even though he did not fight back!" Becoming very angry, Jarāsandha attacked Mathurā seventeen times with very large armies. Kṛṣṇa was thinking, "Should I return to Vraja now?" But He was unable to go, because Vasudeva saw that Kṛṣṇa had not been properly educated; He knew only how to take cows out for grazing. So first he wanted to give Kṛṣṇa the *saṁskāra* of the sacred thread, and for this he called Gargācārya to his home.

Everyone, whether local or from distant places, was invited to the ceremony, but Vrajavāsīs like Nanda and his brother Upananda were intentionally not invited. Taking advice from senior members of the dynasty like Uddhava and Akrūra, Vasudeva and Devakī had decided before in the assembly of

Ugrasena that, "If the residents of Vraja are invited here for the ceremony, then the *bhāva* of Vraja will be stimulated inside Kṛṣṇa and He will certainly desire to return to Vraja with them. If that *bhāva* awakens inside Him, none of us will be able to check it, and therefore it is better not to invite them." For the ceremony, Kṛṣṇa had His head shaved, leaving only a *śikhā*. Wearing wooden sandals and taking a staff, He assumed the full dress of a *brahmacārī*. Then Gargamuni gave Him the *gāyatrī-mantra* and the sacred thread, and putting the cloth for begging alms around His neck, said, "My dear son, now beg some alms."

Previously, in Vraja, Yaśodā had told Kṛṣṇa, "When You receive the sacred thread, we will fill Your begging cloth with jewels." Now Kṛṣṇa remembered that occasion, and in that great assembly He anxiously started looking in all directions, "Where is My mother?" At the ceremony, Devakī was fully decorated in her best attire, sitting in the front to give Kṛṣṇa alms. And Kṛṣṇa was anxiously looking around, "Where is My mother? Where is My mother?" But not seeing her, acute remembrance of Yaśodā came to Him, and He thought, "My mother, somewhere in Nanda-bhavana, will be standing alone by the door. Sometimes she will be looking inside the house, and sometimes she will be looking outside. She will be crying, not knowing where I am and wondering, 'What is my son doing at this moment?' And here I am, accepting this sacred thread amidst a joyous celebration."

Crying out, "*Mother! Mother!*" Kṛṣṇa fell to the ground, unconscious. All of the excitement of the occasion and the giving and taking of alms immediately stopped, and everyone ran to Kṛṣṇa and lifted Him up. Witnessing this spectacle, the members of the Yadu dynasty said, "Just see how strong His attachment is to Vraja! He should be sent far away for His education! He should be sent to Ujjain, and there He can start strictly following His vows and the instructions of His spiritual master. He will stay there as long as the *guru* sees fit, and then upon returning here, His nature will have changed, and He will understand that He is really the son of Vasudeva." So they sent Him there.

Somehow the Vrajavāsīs came to know of all this and said, "Considering Him to be their own son, they have given Him the sacred thread? Forcibly they have made Him a *kṣatriya* through the sacred thread ceremony? And they have cruelly sent Him to Ujjain to receive His education from Sāndīpani Muni? Wearing horizontal markings on his forehead, Sāndīpani Muni is an impersonalist worshipper of Śaṅkara! Why have they sent Kṛṣṇa to *him*?" Yogamāyā had made the arrangement that Kṛṣṇa be sent to Sāndīpani, because if He had been sent to a Vaiṣṇava, the Vaiṣṇava would have recognised Him. Therefore He was sent to a devotee of Śiva who would not recognise Him, and His identity would not be revealed. Kṛṣṇa was sent to Ujjain, and in sixty-four days He learned sixty-four arts.

When Kṛṣṇa returned from there, He sent Uddhava to Vraja. After speaking with Uddhava, one of the *gopīs* began speaking to a bee, considering it to also be a messenger from Kṛṣṇa:

api bata madhu-puryām ārya-putro 'dhunāste
smarati sa pitṛ-gehān saumya bandhūṁś ca gopān
kvacid api sa kathā naḥ kiṅkarīṇāṁ gṛṇīte
bhujam aguru-sugandhaṁ mūrdhny adhāsyat kadā nu

Śrīmad-Bhāgavatam (10.47.21)

Now that Kṛṣṇa has completed His studies at the *āśrama* of Sāndīpani, will He be coming here? Certainly He won't be able to stay in Mathurā! Is He on the road coming here right now? He told Me over two months ago that He will be returning 'the day after tomorrow', but still He has not come. Does He ever remember us at any time? Does He remember us as those who string wonderful flower garlands for Him? Does He remember, 'Oh, the *gopīs'* beauty defeats that of even the most beautiful women in the world!'? Does He ever remember us in that way? Or does He remember us even in a derogatory manner? 'Oh, yes, those *gopīs* are foolish girls who work with milk products and don't know anything.' When He hears a song or sees some dancing, does He remember us and the sentiments we shared, the love of His insignificant *dāsīs*? When will He return and make us fearless by placing His *aguru*-scented hands on our heads, and putting His long arms around our necks as He did during the *rāsa-līlā*?"

Similarly, Nanda Bābā and all the residents of Vraja had extremely strong feelings for Kṛṣṇa from His very childhood, and although He didn't send them any news from Mathurā or Dvārakā, in the end, when it was the appropriate time for *sūrya-pūjā* at Kurukṣetra after the war there, without being called, Nanda Bābā, Yaśodā, the *gopīs* and all the residents of Vraja went there and at last met Him again.

In the verse we are discussing, it says *sva-putram*. The word *sva,* meaning "one's own", is used because otherwise the word *putra* could mean that Kṛṣṇa was the adopted son of Nanda. So this verse says, "Taking his own son" – not taking the son of Vasudeva – "he repeatedly embraced and kissed Him." And because of his great affection for Kṛṣṇa, Nanda experienced *paramam*, that supreme spiritual ecstasy which even Vasudeva never felt. Or another meaning of *paramaṁ mudam* can be that Nanda felt that ecstasy which even Mahā-Lakṣmī, who is worshipful to all devotees, could not attain.

Udāra-dhīḥ – Nanda Bābā was very generous and magnanimous. On the day of Kṛṣṇa's birth festival, he gave cows, jewels, cloth and everything he had in charity to the *brāhmaṇas*. *Udāra* can also mean greatly intelligent. If he hadn't been highly intelligent, he wouldn't have asked Brahmā only for the boon of having that most elevated *vātsalya-prema* for Bhagavān. He didn't ask for an ordinary son, nor did he even ask to have Bhagavān as his son, but he asked only for *bhagavad-bhakti*. This is the proper yearning – begging for *bhakti*, for *prema*. The *ācāryas* in our *sampradāya* don't consider that obtaining Kṛṣṇa is the ultimate objective; they consider that obtaining *kṛṣṇa-prema* is the ultimate objective. Especially the *kṛṣṇa-prema* of the Vrajavāsīs, and within that, especially the *prema* of the *gopīs*. And within that, the *prema* of Rādhā has been emphasised – to have *prema* for Kṛṣṇa as Rādhā-vallabha.

Nanda begged only for *bhagavad-bhakti*, not for having a son. Vasudeva prayed, "We desire a son like You" but Nanda prayed, "We desire to have *vātsalya-prema* for You." When Brahmā had offered the boon to Droṇa and Dharā, Droṇa said, "Please first ask my wife what she desires." Dharā replied, "When Parabrahma Himself takes birth in this world and performs His wonderful human-like pastimes, we desire to have great devotion for Him."

Both a mother and father will love their son, but the mother will love him more. The mother actually nurtures the child, while the father provides all the necessities such as clothing and food. If during the night the father's sleep is broken by the child's crying for even one moment, he may desire to even put the child outside of the house! But the mother will stay awake all night if necessary feeding the child milk, comforting him and lulling him back to sleep. The mother is ready to face any hardship, and therefore she looks after the child in a way that is not possible for the father.

Nanda once went to Mathurā to meet with Vasudeva concerning the taxes which had to be given to Kaṁsa, and one full day elapsed before he returned to Vraja. But Yaśodā couldn't tolerate being away from Kṛṣṇa for even one moment, and therefore Yaśodā's affection for Kṛṣṇa was greater than that of Nanda. When Uddhava visited Vraja, Nanda Bābā was able to converse with him a little, but Yaśodā could not. She couldn't possibly have spoken in her condition; she was simply lying on the ground nearby and bitterly weeping.

When Brahmā stole the cowherd boys and calves, Kṛṣṇa assumed all of their forms for one year and drank the milk of the motherly *gopīs* and cows. Describing the glories of those motherly *gopīs* and cows is very difficult, so what to speak of describing the glories of Yaśodā? With great *prema* she fed Kṛṣṇa milk for the entire time He was residing in Vṛndāvana, and her glories are unlimited and unfathomable. If someone attains even a small particle of *bhakti* for Kṛṣṇa, then they feel that their lives have become completely fulfilled. So what to speak of Yaśodā? I don't know if we even have the courage to attempt to describe her *bhakti*.

After Kṛṣṇa left Vṛndāvana for Mathurā, Mother Yaśodā stopped doing all housework. The kitchen remained unclean, all the pots were upside-down and there were cobwebs everywhere. Who would she cook for? When Kṛṣṇa was present, with great delight she would cook for Him, but she felt that with Kṛṣṇa gone there was no one to cook for. She began displaying the characteristics of someone who is approaching old age, and on one very hot afternoon, when she was feeling particularly unhappy, remembrance of so many of Kṛṣṇa's childhood pastimes began coming to her, and she was at once submerged in *bhāva*. Inside the house were Kṛṣṇa's clothing and many of His toys, like toy cows and tiny bamboo flutes. She collected all of these in a cloth sack and leaving the house, began to walk away. Then one of her friends who lived nearby approached her and said, "*Sakhī*, where are you going?" Seeing that she was going somewhere, others gathered around her and asked, "Mother, where are you going?" Previously she was unable to even speak; whenever she would desire to speak, she would just become choked up with emotion and could only cry. But now she said, "I am going to wherever my Kanhaiyā is."

"What? Where is your Kanhaiyā? This is Nandagrāma, and He is in Mathurā! It is an extremely hot afternoon, the hot sun is bearing down, and the ground will certainly burn your feet, so how will you go anywhere?"

"I cannot live without Him."

"So going to Mathurā, then what will you do?"

"I will go there, and arriving in the reception room, I will say, 'I desire to meet Queen Devakī.' And if someone brings me to Devakī, then I will fall at her feet and say, 'I will become your maidservant birth after birth. I will serve your child – He is not my child – and I will cook for you both. I will become your maidservant for all time. Please keep me in your palace, where I will eat only your remnants and always serve you. That is all I desire.'" Saying that, she became overwhelmed with emotion and fell down right there; she had that much love for the Lord as her son!

The Vraja devotees have the highest level of love for Kṛṣṇa. Their love never comes and goes as the love in this world does; they are all eternal associates of Kṛṣṇa, and their *prema* is like a fathomless ocean. On rainy days, even though the rivers swell and flow even stronger towards the ocean, the ocean itself never swells. And on dry days it never diminishes; so for the fathomless ocean, swelling and diminishing never occurs. It is the same with the love of these devotees, and Nanda and Yaśodā's *prema* for Kṛṣṇa is always taking new and variegated forms.

Chapter Thirteen

Mother Yaśodā Binds Kṛṣṇa

sa mātuḥ svinna-gātrāya
visrasta-kavara-srajaḥ
dṛṣṭvā pariśramaṁ kṛṣṇaḥ
kṛpayāsīt sva-bandhane

Śrīmad-Bhāgavatam (10.9.18); *Bṛhad-bhāgavatāmṛta* (2.7.129)

When Kṛṣṇa saw Yaśodā labouring so desperately that her whole body was dripping with perspiration and the flower garland that was entwined in her hair braid was falling down, He mercifully allowed Himself to be bound by her.

Sanātana Gosvāmī says that in describing the life of Yaśodā, Śukadeva Gosvāmī became joyful and astonished. The *vātsalya* of Yaśodā is more special than anyone else's, and even more special than Nanda's because Kṛṣṇa is not completely overpowered by anyone else's parental affection the way He is by hers. Kṛṣṇa is the one who unties the bindings of this material universe, even for those who approach Him in the mood of an enemy. He is the giver of the five types of *mukti*, liberation: *sālokya* (residing on the same planet as the Lord), *sāmīpya* (becoming His personal associate), *sārūpya* (obtaining a spiritual form similar to His), *sārṣṭi* (obtaining opulence similar to His) and *sāyujya* (merging into His effulgence). Over and above these He gives the special type of liberation known as *prema*. That *prema* He gave even to Pūtanā, who approached Him in the guise of a mother to kill

Him. She was given a motherly position in Goloka even though she was an enemy, and her relatives Aghāsura and Bakāsura, even though they were also enemies, were given *sālokya*. Yet here we find that very giver of liberation Himself being bound by Yaśodā; just see what a pastime this is!

Outside her house beneath a large pot filled with milk, Yaśodā lit a fire fuelled by cow-dung, and the smoke was rising in all directions. Then she returned to churning butter. It was early morning, the day after Dīpāvalī, and while going about their morning duties, all of the household servants were remembering and singing about Kṛṣṇa's pastimes. At that time Kṛṣṇa woke up, and not seeing His mother, He got up from His bed and began crying loudly. When Yaśodā looked over and saw the small, naked boy, she took Him in her lap and began to feed Him milk. At that time, she felt such strong waves of spiritual ecstasy that tears fell from her eyes and milk came to her breasts. There was not even any need for Kṛṣṇa to suck the milk out; automatically it flowed and Kṛṣṇa drank without effort.

Meanwhile Yaśodā saw that the milk she had placed on the fire was boiling over, so she immediately got up and ran there. Before she wanted only to take Kṛṣṇa in her lap and feed Him, yet now her immediate concern was the milk – it was boiling over and would not wait. At that moment she was not thinking about whether Kṛṣṇa was satisfied or not, and even though Kṛṣṇa was grasping her with both His hands and His mouth, leaving Him behind she got up to see to the milk. The powerful *rākṣasī* Pūtanā tried desperately to escape the grasp of that same Kṛṣṇa, but could not. She even flew into the sky and tried to fly back to Mathurā, but Kṛṣṇa clutched her breast with such ferocity that she fell to the ground. Effortlessly Kṛṣṇa was able to hold onto Pūtanā, yet when Kṛṣṇa desired that "Mother will not leave Me!" and He even applied all of His *śakti*, still she went to look after the milk and left Him sitting there. Becoming very angry, Kṛṣṇa began crying and His eyes became red. Biting His lip as children do, He thought, "Mother left Me and didn't feed Me milk?" and He picked up a stone and broke the butter pot.

Yaśodā was saying to the milk, "Don't boil over! I need you to prepare sweets for Kṛṣṇa!" But the milk may have been feeling, "What do you need me for? What is the nature of Kṛṣṇa's stomach? It can never really be filled. But neither can your milk supply ever be exhausted; Kṛṣṇa could keep drinking it forever and it would never run out. Therefore my own life is worthless. If I will never be able to satisfy Kṛṣṇa, then I will give up my life by boiling over into the fire."

Seeing that the milk had risen and was boiling over, Yaśodā said to it, "Don't give up your life! I need you to prepare sweets for Kṛṣṇa!" After sprinkling some water on the milk to prevent it from boiling over, Yaśodā returned and found the broken butter pot. Not seeing Kṛṣṇa, she searched and searched until she noticed His footprints leading in the direction of the house, and she laughed to herself as she saw Him feeding some yoghurt to the monkeys and taking some Himself. She thought, "Kṛṣṇa is a real friend of these monkeys! I should discipline Him for this, but it would spoil the fun. And besides, until now I have not done such a thing." So laughing a little, she picked up a stick to frighten Him and quietly hid so He wouldn't know she was watching. She thought, "If He looks this way and comes to know that I am watching, then I will have to at once run to catch Him." And Kṛṣṇa was also alert, thinking, "If Mother or anyone comes, I must run away at once."

Yaśodā saw that there was a group of crows there along with the monkeys. All of them were previously in *rāma-līlā* – the crows were from the dynasty of Kākabhuśaṇḍi, and the monkeys were from the dynasty of Hanumān and Sugrīva. Kṛṣṇa was indebted to all of them, so He was feeding them. The crows were below catching the drops of yoghurt that fell to the ground, and the monkeys were beside Kṛṣṇa taking the yoghurt directly with their hands. At first she laughed, but then, very slowly, like a cat, she approached Him, and He – whose very name pushes away the influence of *māyā* for the people of this world and saves them from seeing the Yamadūtas – looked at her with fearful eyes. Who could He be afraid of? Was He afraid of Kaṁsa? Some say that He went to Gokula out of fear of Kaṁsa, but really He went there to taste *prema*. He is never afraid of anyone, yet upon seeing Yaśodā, He jumped down and ran off.

Yaśodā ran after Him, and we also desire to catch Bhagavān by our *bhakti*, yet unlike her, we cannot catch Him. "So many days have passed, and every day I have engaged in chanting *harināma*. Yet as of today I still have no direct experience of Bhagavān. My heart has not melted and I have never shed tears for Him, and I have never felt ecstasy while chanting the holy name. How will my heart become changed? I can see no light at the end of the tunnel or anything. How will I ever attain *bhakti*?" We should consider these things. As long as even a little mundane vision remains within us, we won't be able to catch Him. By realisation of the subtle plane we won't catch Him, and by realisation of the *nirguṇa* plane we won't catch Him. Our mentality must be like that of the Vrajavāsīs such as Yaśodā and the other *gopīs*, and then we will be able to catch Him; otherwise not. But we are also running after Him; we also possess some eagerness. Perhaps we have performed some sacrifice in the service of our spiritual master and when we hear *hari-kathā* we get some devotional feelings, but do we possess that *prema* which overpowers Bhagavān? Even the pure-hearted *yogīs* in their *samādhi* cannot catch a glimpse of the Lord's shadow!

Yaśodā is *really* giving chase to Kṛṣṇa – on foot, not by the speed of mind. That is another thing. She is not pursuing Him by the speed of mind but on foot, and trying to catch Kṛṣṇa in His manifest form. Sometimes she would come near Him, and again He would give her the slip, and like this He was playing with His mother. If we possessed such *bhakti* by which we could come near Kṛṣṇa, then would it be easy to catch Him? It would still be very difficult. Even in "coming near Him", how far away would we still be? Even though He is always near, present inside our hearts, we are not seeing Him there. Yaśodā sees Him, chases after Him, and catches Him, but what about us? We don't perform the required *sādhana* or *bhajana* to catch Him. We will only catch Him when we have sufficient eagerness within us, but first the urges for mundane pleasure must be completely forgotten. Kṛṣṇa is running and Yaśodā is also running, but she will have to run twice as fast as Kṛṣṇa to catch Him.

Sugrīva's brother Vāli worshipped the sun-god Sūrya by performing austerities, and then Sūrya appeared before him and asked, "What boon do you desire?" Vāli said, "I desire the boon that whenever anyone comes before me to fight, I will keep all of my own strength and also take half of my opponent's strength." One day after having received this boon, Vāli was at a river offering *pūjā* to Sūryadeva when the demon Rāvaṇa approached him. Rāvaṇa thought that he was the strongest person in the entire universe, and with his twenty hands began disturbing Vāli by splashing water on him. But Vāli simply continued offering his *pūjā* with only one hand and with the other he grabbed hold of Rāvaṇa and held him underneath his armpit. Vāli didn't even look at Rāvaṇa, like one who has killed a mosquito on his back.

Besides Bhagavān no one could kill Vāli, and even then, Bhagavān had to use some trickery to kill him. Rāma killed him from a hidden position. Otherwise, if He had gone before Vāli, Vāli would have taken half of His strength and Rāma would have also been defeated! In a similar way, we can see that for catching Kṛṣṇa, double speed is necessary; then He can be caught. "Double speed" means that our own sincere efforts must be there, and Kṛṣṇa's mercy must also be upon us. He loves all *jīvas*, but *we* must love *Him* twice as much, and then we can catch Him.

Sometimes Kṛṣṇa remembers His own *bhagavattā* (nature as the Supreme), but all the time Yaśodā loves Him with the idea that He is merely an ordinary child, and she gives her everything to Him. In this stage of *prema* there may appear to be even more affection for the beloved's possessions than for the beloved himself. We may have great devotion to our father, but then if we put on our father's sandals and wear them ourselves, is that real devotion, or not? We should respect the sandals of our father as much as we respect him, just as Bharata served the wooden sandals of Rāmacandra. That is the correct outlook, that is really *prema*. But if we are indifferent to the possessions of our beloved that is not *prema*, and if we use them for our own enjoyment that is not *prema*. Kṛṣṇa's cloth, His flute, His toys, milk and butter that are meant for Him – a real devotee will sometimes appear to have more love for these things because they are dear to Kṛṣṇa.

With great love Yaśodā feeds Kṛṣṇa milk, so does she have more affection for Kṛṣṇa Himself, or for the milk? Of course for Kṛṣṇa, but if the milk becomes spoiled in some way, she will be very upset. She thinks, "If Kṛṣṇa takes this milk, He will live a long, healthy life. From this milk I will make *sandeśa*, *rabarī*, *khīra*, *malpura* and so many delectable preparations to feed Kṛṣṇa." At other times, when Mother Yaśodā makes Kṛṣṇa some beautiful new silken clothes and after dressing Him in them He goes outside and plays in some nearby mud, then, seeing Him, Yaśodā says, "Hey! Look what you've done to Your new clothes!" Then Kṛṣṇa thinks, "Does Mother have more love for Me, or for My *clothes*?" Therefore devotees may sometimes show even more regard for Kṛṣṇa's paraphernalia than for Kṛṣṇa Himself; that is one symptom of *prema*. And what are Kṛṣṇa's dearest possessions but His devotees? This is why even after performing *bhajana* for thousands of lifetimes those who don't respect His devotees will attain absolutely nothing.

Therefore Yaśodā went to protect the milk so that it would not be wasted, and when Kṛṣṇa broke the butter pot, she ran after Him to correct Him. Lifting her stick, she said, "All right – now I will hit You!"

Frightened, Kṛṣṇa replied, "Mother, don't hit Me!"

"Tell me then – why did You break the pot?"

"I didn't break it!"

"Then who did?"

"You must have accidentally broken it as you ran by! You were not completely to your senses!"

Then Yaśodā became more angry and said, "And why are You stealing? There are no thieves on my side of the family! You are the only thief in our family!" Again Kṛṣṇa ran off, and again she lifted up her stick and chased Him. As she was running, her hair loosened and she was becoming fatigued, but she was determined to catch Him. Finally with the help of some of the household servants He was caught, and she brought Him inside the house. "Now shall I hit You, restless friend of the monkeys? You steal from the homes of others as well as Your own house! Do You think that's good?"

Kṛṣṇa replied, "Mother, don't hit Me! There is no purpose in hitting Me!"

So she put down the stick and said, "All right, I will bind You instead." So she took the rope from her loosened hair and tried to bind Him. His thin waist was so nicely decorated with golden ornaments, and applying the rope to it, she found that the rope was short. She said to the *gopīs*, "Bring more rope!" But even upon more rope being added, Kṛṣṇa still could not be bound. Yogamāyā saw that, "My master does not desire to be bound now." Therefore Kṛṣṇa's waist remained the same size, but by the influence of Yogamāyā the rope was always two finger lengths short. Because she still did not have sufficient determination, Yaśodā couldn't wrap it all the way around even once, and everyone was astonished.

What difficulty should there be in binding such a thin waist? It is like those of us who are presently practising *sādhana-bhajana*. In general we believe that Bhagavān is very merciful, but sometimes our faith becomes weak. "Is there really so much *śakti* in the name of Bhagavān, or not? Can it really bestow *bhakti*, or not? Will I ever meet Bhagavān?" If in the midst of the process of chanting *harināma* all of one's difficulties are not eradicated, he may begin to think, "Is Bhagavān there, or not?" He may feel that he has attained nothing, that his unhappiness has not been mitigated, his poverty has not been eradicated, and after doing *bhajana* his whole life, he may merely die crying in disappointment. Rather we should continue chanting with such good quality faith that we will always be thinking, "My endeavour will certainly be successful."

But sometimes our determination is not firm, and many *sādhakas* fall into the trap of again becoming involved in enjoying *māyā*, thinking, "I will work hard, make lots of money, build a house and live comfortably," but they forget that one day they will have to die and leave it all behind. At first Yaśodā thought that she would easily wrap the rope around Kṛṣṇa's waist, but did it happen? Similarly, when we first take up devotional life we think that attaining Bhagavān will not be difficult; but recognising the reality of it, we should never become despondent. Many devotees become despondent, but we should always remain eager and determined.

After some time, the *gopīs* were wonderstruck, and especially Yaśodā's astonishment knew no limit as they saw that thousands of ropes had been joined together but still this small child could not be bound. Yaśodā thought, "From early morning until now I have been trying to bind Him! The rope has become so long, and still it won't wrap around Him even once. Every time it is two finger lengths short. Not one, three, four or five finger lengths short, but every time it is precisely two finger lengths short! Why is this?"

There were two reasons for the rope being short. First, Yogamāyā saw that Kṛṣṇa did not desire to be bound, so Kṛṣṇa's sanction was not present, and second, there was not sufficient eagerness in Yaśodā. There is the mercy of Kṛṣṇa and a devotee's eagerness for *bhajana.* When they both come together, one will meet Bhagavān and overpower Him with *prema.* As long as Yaśodā was not sufficiently eager, she could not bind Him. But then she became more determined, thinking, "This is my own small child, and standing before all of my friends I am unable to bind Him? Now I will certainly bind Him, or else I might as well give up my life!" She began perspiring and her face became red, and *kṛpayāsīt sva-bandhane* – seeing her endeavour to bind Him, Kṛṣṇa's heart melted. The influence of Yogamāyā withdrew, and at last He allowed her to bind Him.

Sanātana Gosvāmī says here that there are two types of devotees: those who desire to attain Bhagavān by the practice of *sādhana-bhajana*, and those who rely solely on Kṛṣṇa's mercy. Mahāprabhu said that both are necessary. Kittens don't need to make any effort; the cat feeds them and nurtures them and carries them everywhere in her mouth, and all the kittens do all day and night is merely cry "*meow, meow*". But baby monkeys have to hold onto their mothers themselves; otherwise they will be finished. When the mother is ready to cross from one roof or tree to another, at once the baby monkey runs over and holds on around her stomach or on her back and is carried across. She never grabs the babies herself, and if they don't grab onto her, she goes without them, thinking, "What good are such useless offspring anyway?"

So which is the primary consideration here concerning *sādhana* or *kṛpā*, mercy? Mahāprabhu said that both are essential. No one can actually bind Bhagavān by the strength of their *sādhana*, but by endeavouring more and more until such great determination comes that all of one's bodily needs and worldly attachments are forgotten, then Bhagavān's heart will melt and He will bestow special mercy. Bhagavān's *kṛpā* is upon all living entities at all times, but not that special mercy by which He can actually be bound. He only gives that upon seeing the intense endeavour of His devotees, like the renunciation of Raghunātha dāsa Gosvāmī. How did he perform *bhajana*, day and night? The Six Gosvāmīs would live outdoors in the jungle, such as at Nandagrāma, or near Pāvana-sarovara, where a cool breeze is always blowing. They would reside beneath trees, and nearby were snakes, scorpions and many different kinds of jungle animals. They ate very little and performed extremely strict *bhajana*.

By that kind of *bhajana* one can meet Bhagavān, but where is such strictness and intensity in our *bhajana*? With great comfort we are eating and drinking, and we possess quilts, pillows and shawls. On cold days we have plenty of hot food to eat, and there is never any deficiency in our sleeping. Therefore Bhagavān's mercy is upon us, the mercy of the Vaiṣṇavas is upon us, but it is our misfortune that we don't have the same intensity as the Six Gosvāmīs.

Wonderstruck and experiencing ecstatic symptoms in his description of the glories of Yaśodā, next Śukadeva Gosvāmī experienced these feelings arising in his heart:

nemaṁ viriñco na bhavo
na śrīr apy aṅga-saṁśrayā
prasādaṁ lebhire gopī
yat tat prāpa vimuktidāt

Śrīmad-Bhāgavatam (10.9.20); *Bṛhad-bhāgavatāmṛta* (2.7.130)

Neither Brahmā, Śiva or even Lakṣmī-devī – who eternally resides at Kṛṣṇa's chest in the form of a golden line – have ever received as much mercy as Yaśodā did from He who is the bestower of liberation.

Although being Bhagavān's own son, still, even Brahmā didn't attain as much mercy as Yaśodā did. Brahmā was born from the lotus of Bhagavān's navel. Generally a father is most munificent to his son regardless of the son's nature – whether he is a criminal or whatever. And usually the son is made the father's heir in all respects, but even such a highly qualified son as Brahmā did not receive the mercy which Yaśodā did. Coming to Vraja, Brahmā saw, "First this offender Aghāsura tried to swallow Kṛṣṇa, and then I saw Kṛṣṇa give liberation to him! I saw a light leave Aghāsura's body, fly up into the sky, and then merge into Kṛṣṇa's feet! That was no ordinary light; it was certainly Aghāsura's soul!"

Many were not able to recognise the divine symptoms of Kṛṣṇa and only saw Him as an ordinary human being. As Kṛṣṇa prepared to leave this world and return to Goloka in His form as Dvārakādhīśa, what did the ordinary people see? That Kṛṣṇa was shot by a hunter's arrow, He began to bleed and He died right there. Others saw a light come out of Kṛṣṇa's body and go into the sky. Brahmā, Śaṅkara and others saw Kṛṣṇa return to Goloka in His selfsame form as His eternal associates offered Him prayers. And what did the higher devotees of Dvārakā see? That Kṛṣṇa didn't go anywhere; He always remains in Dvārakā. So according to their different levels of inner development, people saw Him in different ways.

When Brahmā saw Kṛṣṇa's pastime of giving liberation to Aghāsura, he became very astonished and thought, "How can I see more pastimes like this?" Meanwhile, Kṛṣṇa remembered that He wanted to Himself become all of those cowherd boys and calves, so here was the opportunity to accomplish all of His objectives in one pastime. In this pastime He could marry all of the *gopīs*, because if He had kept relationships with them otherwise, the people of mundane consciousness would have criticised Him. Next Yogamāyā sent inspiration into the heart of Brahmā and he thought, "Let me see what will happen next if I steal the cowherd boys and calves."

In the end, seeing how Kṛṣṇa Himself expanded into all of the cowherd boys and calves, how all of their sticks and blankets and everything appeared as four-armed Nārāyaṇas, and how so many demigods were offering them prayers, he became wonderstruck and immediately fell down like a stick at Kṛṣṇa's feet. Then he looked again, and everything had disappeared, and only the original form of Kṛṣṇa remained, standing in His threefold-bending posture and smiling.

Na-bhavaḥ – Śaṅkara also did not receive as much mercy as Yaśodā did. And who is Śaṅkara? He and Hari are one and the same soul. For the purpose of showing the ideal standard of worshipping Śaṅkara to the residents of this world, Kṛṣṇa once worshipped Śaṅkara. Brahmā may become offended, but Śaṅkara never accepts any offence. And Kṛṣṇa assigns Śaṅkara very difficult tasks, even up to bewildering the *jīvas* in his incarnation as Śaṅkarācārya and Śaṅkara always fulfils those tasks. Therefore he is certainly the recipient of Kṛṣṇa's mercy, but not the *prasāda*, the special mercy that is spoken of in this verse.

Na śrīḥ – and not even Lakṣmī, who always resides at the Lord's chest and who performed austerities and *pūjā* at Baelvana, received such mercy as Yaśodā did. *Vimuktidāt* – Kṛṣṇa is the giver of liberation. He bestows upon some the destination of Vaikuṇṭha, and upon others even the destination of Goloka Vṛndāvana, but to Yaśodā He gave that special mercy which was not given to anyone else and by which He Himself becomes bound.

Chapter Fourteen

Pūrva-rāga, or Preliminary Attraction

gopīnāṁ paramānanda
āsīd govinda-darśane
kṣaṇaṁ yuga-śatam iva
yāsāṁ yena vinābhavat

Śrīmad-Bhāgavatam (10.19.16); *Bṛhad-bhāgavatāmṛta* (2.7.133)

The *vraja-gopīs* would enjoy supreme pleasure from receiving the *darśana* of Śrī Govinda, but they would consider even one moment of His absence to be like one hundred *yugas*.

Kṛṣṇa and the *sakhās* had taken the cows out to graze in the Muñjāraṇya forest when a fire started, and like a chariot driver the wind carried that fire until it surrounded the boys and cows on all sides. Then the *sakhās* called out, "Kṛṣṇa! Baladeva! Save us!" Seeing that they were threatened, Kṛṣṇa said, "Just close your eyes!" and He opened His mouth and consumed the fierce fire. Then He told them that they could open their eyes; if they had witnessed His swallowing that great fire they would have been terrified. But the *sakhās* saw that everything was just as it was before and that the cows were calmly resting under the Bhāṇḍīra tree. They thought, "How is it that we are here? Everything was just burning! Was that just a dream, or was it real?" And then they all began blissfully taking their lunch together.

In the same way, when by the cultivation of *bhagavad-bhajana* and the mercy of the spiritual master and Bhagavān we become free from the burning suffering of the material energy, we will think, "Was it just a dream, or was it real?" Upon the eradication of that pain which had been tormenting us since time immemorial, we will think, "Where has it gone, as if in the snap of a finger? Was it real?" We really won't be able to remember.

After this Kṛṣṇa led the cows back to Vraja, and the *gopīs* were thirsty for His *darśana*, and that is the time being described in this verse spoken by Śukadeva Gosvāmī. When He came before them, their *ānanda* increased. Although they had not yet established a relationship with Him through either seeing Him or hearing about Him, they were very attracted to Him, and this is called *pūrva-rāga*. It can exist in both the *viṣaya*, the supreme object of love, Kṛṣṇa, and in the *āśraya*, the supreme receptacle of love, the *gopīs*.

To feel this *pūrva-rāga* in the stage of *sādhana* is not easy; the *pūrva-rāga* that has been described in the writings of Vidyāpati, Caṇḍīdāsa and in the *Gopī-gīta* and other places in the *Śrīmad-Bhāgavatam* cannot be attained by an ordinary *sādhaka*. Only when one has attained *svarūpa-siddhi* – meaning when in the stage of *bhāva* one attains perception of his eternal identity – will such restlessness for the sight of Kṛṣṇa be felt. Only a very few devotees, like Bilvamaṅgala, have felt these kind of sentiments in the selfsame lifetime. But *kṣaṇaṁ yuga-śatam iva* – feeling a moment of Kṛṣṇa's absence to be like millenniums – what is the nature of this sentiment? Although here it is *pūrva-rāga*, it can also be *mahābhāva*, as in this verse:

yugāyitaṁ nimeṣeṇa
cakṣuṣā prāvṛṣāyitam
śūnyāyitaṁ jagat sarvaṁ
govinda-viraheṇa me

Śrī Śikṣāṣṭaka (7)

O *sakhī*, in separation from Govinda, even one second seems like millenniums. Tears are flowing from My eyes like clouds showering torrents of rain, and the entire world appears empty.

This is also *mahābhāva*; it is not an ordinary sentiment. The poet Caṇḍīdāsa has written:

sai! kevā sunāile śyāma nāma?
kānera bhitara diyā, marame pasila go,
ākula karila mora prāṇa

Although outwardly it is on the order of Nanda and Yaśodā that Kṛṣṇa joins the other boys to take the cows out to graze for the day – He knows this is the *dharma* for those of His class – it is actually with immense *bhāva* that He joins His friends. He has just passed His *paugaṇḍa* age and is entering His *kaiśora* age. Kṛṣṇa is speaking with Subala or some other cowherd boy, and the *sakhīs* are conversing amongst themselves. *Sai* is a very simple and sweet word for *sakhī*. They say, "*Sai*, why have we been made to hear the name of Śyāma? Entering through our ears, it has touched the core of our hearts and confounded our very lives."

At once the *gopīs* became perplexed in the eagerness to attain Kṛṣṇa, and *this* is the very purpose of hearing the scriptures. By hearing the glories of our worshipful deity through the medium of our ears, our heart should become so attached to Him that day and night we will do nothing besides meditate on His sweetness. The *gopīs* have not just come to the end of *sādhana* by attaining *svarūpa-siddhi*, but they are actually manifestations of the *hlādinī-śakti*. This meditation is not possible for ordinary people. But as men who work in an oil factory will certainly develop a coating of oil on their hands, similarly when a *sādhaka* hears and speaks about these topics, "his hands will become coated", meaning that a little *bhāva* will arise in him by which his life will become successful.

Our spiritual sentiments should be so deep that we won't be able to forget them even for a moment, but regrettably, we have become accustomed to generally doing exactly the opposite. We hear these topics, but it seems as if immediately afterwards, remembrance of material enjoyment consumes us. We are chanting the holy name, studying *ślokas* and giving scriptural readings, but where are our minds? Just as when we place an empty pot in a river it immediately fills up with water, immediately after hearing some of this *bhagavat-kathā* our minds will again become filled with thoughts of the sense enjoyment that we have been experiencing since time immemorial. We must try to keep the mind free from these thoughts, even though it may not always remain steady. We should go to wherever *hari-kathā* is being spoken and completely fill our minds with it, leaving no room for thoughts of sense enjoyment.

Indeed, there is nothing more favourable for us than hearing *hari-kathā*, and it should be as our food. We should have love for *hari-kathā*, and if not, then we should at least consider it our duty to hear it, understanding that it will bestow upon us our ultimate good fortune. Those whose hearts have been thoroughly purified, who never think of sense enjoyment – when they hear such *kathā*, deep sentiments that touch the very core of their hearts arise, and they remain absorbed in those sentiments day and night.

In another place Caṇḍīdāsa writes that the young *kiśorī* daughter of Mahārāja Vṛṣabhānu sits alone, completely perplexed, not speaking to anyone, and one of Her elders says to Her, "My child, what are You doing? Why are You sitting there like that? Come over here and do this task." But She doesn't listen; She is unable to comprehend what has happened inside Her. Her eyes are open, which is a symptom of consciousness, but She isn't looking at anything. She saw Śyāma one time, but He left, and now She just remains silent and motionless. She has no desire to eat, and She is wearing red cloth – why? To help Her forget His bodily complexion so that She won't become more dazed and Her condition won't then be detected by Her elders. With a hair-band She has tied white flowers onto Her hair so that its dark shade will not remind Her of Śyāma, but since He has already captured the core of Her heart, how can She possibly prevent remembrance of Him from coming?

Then She began gazing at a cloud that possessed the same complexion as Śyāma. Sometimes She enters the house and sometimes She comes back out; She takes long breaths and Her mind is not steady on anything. Then an elder says to Her, "Why did You go there? What was the necessity? Beware! Don't ever look in the direction of that boy again! Don't focus Your mind on Him for even one moment, or You won't be able to perform Your household duties! You are not listening to me, so have You now lost the fear of Your elders as well? Has some ghost or demigod possessed You?" Not aware of anything, She falls down, and when they lift Her up and place Her somewhere else, She falls down again. Because She has lost Her fear of Her elders, they even abandon the idea of finding a husband for Her. But Caṇḍīdāsa says, "Yes, I understand: She is not mad, not possessed, nothing of the sort, but She has simply fallen into the trap of that black snake Śyāma." This is *pūrva-rāga*.

But how can a *sādhaka* experience this? Generally our minds are full of unlimited varieties of material desires, but when none of these desires remain, meaning when one obtains the company of an exalted *guru* and receives the unconditional mercy of Bhagavān, then some shadow of *bhāva* will come. By chanting the extraordinarily beautiful *śyāma-nāma* and the Hare Kṛṣṇa *mantra*, Rūpa Gosvāmī, Raghunātha dāsa Gosvāmī and Nārada all went mad in ecstasy, so tell me then – how much *bhāva* must be contained within it? And Bhaktivinoda Ṭhākura also has written so many lines that are saturated with *bhāva*, like:

vibhāvarī-śeṣa, āloka-praveśa,
nidrā chāḍi' uṭha jīva

Kalyāṇa-kalpataru (*Nāma-kīrtana* 2)

This refers to meditating on the pastimes that Kṛṣṇa performs at the end of the night while ordinary *jīvas* remain sleeping. And in the same song, *phula-śara-jojaka kāma*: "Śrī Kṛṣṇa utilises flowered arrows to increase the *gopīs'* desire." Until one has understood well the conception delineated in *Ujjvala-nīlamaṇi*, he won't understand this line. Or if the *kāma-gāyatrī* reveals itself to someone, then that person will understand something of its meaning, but without the mercy of the *kāma-gāyatrī* it cannot be understood. The *bhāva* of a *mahā-bhāgavata* Vaiṣṇava comes within this line, but even though we sing this line every morning, what do *we* accrue from it? Therefore the difference between a *sādhaka's* chanting of the holy name and a perfected soul's chanting of the holy name is like the difference between the land and the sky. When one has fully realised the sweetness of *harināma*, then his tongue will not be able to stop chanting it. For example, when Caitanya Mahāprabhu would go to pass water, He would firmly grasp His tongue with one hand. Seeing this, His young servant Gopāla asked, "O Lord, why are You doing this?"

Mahāprabhu replied, "My tongue doesn't obey Me. One shouldn't take the name of Govinda in a contaminated place, but it won't obey Me."

Gopāla replied, "But my Lord, at the time of dying one may pass stool and urine, and if we don't chant the holy name at that time, our lives will be spoiled!"

Being pleased, Mahāprabhu said, "As of today you have

become *guru*. Yes, the holy name should be taken at that time also." So He released His tongue and chanted at all times, even when going to the bathroom. During the night, Mahāprabhu's servant Govinda dāsa thought that He was merely sleeping, but He would remain awake chanting *kṛṣṇa-nāma*, crying and sometimes rubbing His face on the wall. And when Rāya Rāmānanda and Svarūpa Dāmodara would come, Govinda dāsa would become very unhappy and think, "Why have they come? They will make Him cry and He will not be able to sleep tonight."

When this high type of intense *bhāva* comes while chanting the holy name, then one's composure will be destroyed and he will think, "Without seeing Kṛṣṇa I cannot live any longer! How can I meet Him? What will I do?" Then one's fear of elders, fear of being disgraced in society, and self-restraint are all lost. There are certain inhibitions that restrain love, but when they are all broken down, one's self-restraint is lost. Even Rukmiṇī and Satyabhāmā are not capable of this, so what to speak of others? The night before her proposed marriage, through a *brāhmaṇa* Rukmiṇī sent a message to Kṛṣṇa saying, "Tomorrow I will be married. If You don't come and save me from this, I will give up my life. Shamefully I am writing this to You; a cultured girl should not write like this, but shamefully I am writing to You because otherwise a jackal will snatch away the lion's share." So even though Rukmiṇī is expressing these deep sentiments, she feels some shame; but the *gopīs* feel no such shame, and therefore their *bhāva* is so much deeper. When the *gopīs* would see Kṛṣṇa returning from taking the cows out to graze, they would gaze upon Him with greedy eyes and their *ānanda* would increase. But when they couldn't see Him, even a moment seemed like millions of *yugas* that would never pass. This is *pūrva-rāga*, and countless beautiful sentiments are included within it.

The *gopīs* felt that the time which elapsed during the blinking of their eyes was like an infinity, and they have themselves described this in *Śrīmad-Bhāgavatam* (10.31.15):

aṭati yad bhavān ahni kānanaṁ
truṭi yugāyate tvām apaśyatām
kuṭila-kuntalaṁ śrī-mukhaṁ ca te
jaḍa udīkṣatāṁ pakṣma-kṛd dṛśām

When Kṛṣṇa would spend the day wandering in the forest with the *sakhās*, the *gopīs*, unable to see His beautiful face adorned with lovely locks of hair, would be anguished in separation from Him. And what to speak of that, even when Kṛṣṇa *was* before them, they considered the tiny fraction of time that elapsed in the blinking of their eyes to be like millenniums, and they cursed the creator Brahmā as being foolish for having created eyes that must blink. Our time is mostly spent joking around, but in comparison what kind of *bhajana* was performed by these great personalities?

We have read that only once in his entire life did Raghunātha dāsa Gosvāmī laugh. While he was reading Rūpa Gosvāmī's *Vidagdha-mādhava-nāṭaka*, his tears were falling on the hand-written pages and smearing the ink. Seeing this, Rūpa Gosvāmī asked for it back, but Raghunātha dāsa clutched it to his heart and refused to return it. Therefore Rūpa Gosvāmī composed the *Dāna-keli-kaumudī* very quickly, and after reading only a few verses of it, Raghunātha dāsa began laughing. Otherwise he remained crying for Kṛṣṇa throughout his entire life. If there is such crying for Kṛṣṇa, then that is real *sādhana* and one will certainly receive His *darśana*, just as in the case of Bilvamaṅgala. Presently we may be engaged in only the semblance (*ābhāsa*) of real *sādhana*, but if even in this stage of *sādhana-ābhāsa* we feel so much joy by hearing and speaking this *kathā*, then just imagine how blissful we will feel when we enter into real *sādhana*!

Chapter Fifteen

Kṛṣṇa's Beauty is Unsurpassed

tan-manaskās tad-ālāpās
tad-viceṣṭās tad-ātmikāḥ
tad-guṇān eva gāyantyo
nātmāgārāṇi sasmaruḥ

Śrīmad-Bhāgavatam (10.30.43); *Bṛhad-bhāgavatāmṛta* (2.7.134)

Those *vraja-gopīs,* who had fully given their hearts to Śrī Kṛṣṇa, would imitate His manner of speaking and His activities. Since they had offered their very souls to Him and always sang His glories, they completely forgot themselves and their family interests.

In the gradual development of *bhakti*, from *niṣṭhā* comes *ruci*, where it becomes tasteful. From *ruci* comes *āsakti*, where one will have no desire to leave it. Then comes *bhāva*, and then *prema*, *sneha*, *māna*, *praṇaya*, *rāga*, *anurāga*, and in some cases even *mahābhāva*, where one receives the pinnacle of experience of Kṛṣṇa. Possessing this *mahābhāva*, the *gopīs'* minds and hearts became so absorbed in Kṛṣṇa that they could no longer be considered their own. If you place a piece of cotton on a few drops of water, the water is immediately absorbed into it. Similarly, the water of the *gopīs'* hearts was immediately absorbed into the Kṛṣṇa-cotton in such a way that it was as if their individual existences were lost. If someone is fortunate enough to receive Kṛṣṇa's direct *darśana* or to hear about Him from a *rasika*

Vaiṣṇava, then they may also experience this same absorption. Singing about His virtues more and more, they at once became *tad-ātmikā* – they completely forgot their own bodies, their bodily relations, their homes, everything.

If we have a task to perform but due to some obstacle we cannot complete it, we simply return home. But the *gopīs* were searching for Kṛṣṇa everywhere, asking the vines, trees, *tulasī* and the deer if they had seen Him; still they could not find Him anywhere. But did they return to their homes? Even though they could not find Him, their homes and families had been completely forgotten. They became so absorbed in thinking of Him that it was as if they were possessed by ghosts. Taking on Kṛṣṇa's identity, they began imitating His activities and saying to one another, "How beautiful is my gait? How beautifully do I play the flute?" At that time they didn't know what they were doing, and this is what is meant by the words *tan-manaskāḥ*. They became so absorbed in Kṛṣṇa that their natures changed like iron put into a fire and they forgot everything.

As the *gopīs* searched for Kṛṣṇa, all they remembered were His virtues and His pastimes with them. Whereas we think mostly of our material comforts and are capable of forgetting *bhakti*, they are just the opposite. We should endeavour to become like the eternal associates of Caitanya Mahāprabhu, such as Mādhavendra Purī, who would go days without eating or even begging and was always absorbed in remembrance of Kṛṣṇa. As our *bhakti* increases, we will forget more and more the demands of our bodies and our bodily relations, and this remembrance will also increase. Kṛṣṇa had left the *gopīs*, but they never thought, "Kṛṣṇa is so cruel because He has left us!" Otherwise they would have given up searching for Him and returned home, but they didn't do that. They continued searching for Him, and they began singing in glorification of His virtues, especially His kindness:

praṇata-dehināṁ pāpa-karṣaṇaṁ
tṛṇa-carānugaṁ śrī-niketanam
phaṇi-phaṇārpitaṁ te padāmbujaṁ
kṛṇu kuceṣu naḥ kṛndhi hṛc-chayam

Śrīmad-Bhāgavatam (10.31.7)

O Lord, You are very merciful. Why are You afraid that there may be a sinful reaction if You were to place Your lotus feet on our breasts? By merely remembering Your name, all sins are destroyed.

Praṇata means that if one surrenders everything to Bhagavān including one's false ego, then all sins are destroyed, and when all of one's sins are destroyed, then at once one receives Bhagavān's direct *darśana*. Gajendra the elephant fought with a crocodile for thousands of years until, being partially submerged in water, he took a lotus in his trunk and held it up as an offering to Bhagavān while silently praying, "O Lord, now I am surrendered to You, and I am not even concerned if You save me or if I perish." By the power of this surrender, all of his *anarthas* and *aparādhas* from so many lives were destroyed and at once Bhagavān came. He killed the crocodile with His *cakra*, and Gajendra was released.

If someone factually surrenders to Bhagavān, then that surrender will be the destroyer of all of his faults. Are we surrendered like this? Have all of our faults and offences been eradicated? This is the measuring stick. Most of the suffering that we are feeling and the obstacles that are arising in our *bhajana* are reactions to our misdeeds in previous lives. No matter where one goes, these reactions to previous *karma* and offences cannot be escaped, so an intelligent man will remain in the company of *sādhus* who will gradually lead him to Bhagavān.

The *gopīs* pray, "*praṇata-dehināṁ pāpa-karṣaṇam* – O Govinda, You are so merciful that You destroy the sins of those who surrender to You. We are surrendered to You, so is it that because of the sins of our previous lives You remain hidden from us and do not give us Your *darśana*? We are crying in separation from You, and today, in this world there is no one as unhappy as us. We have abandoned forever our homes and families, and now we are left with no other shelter besides You! So won't You destroy all of our sins?" These are the inner sentiments of one *gopī*. There are so many different kinds of *gopīs* with different sentiments, and another *gopī* is saying, "You destroy the sins of one who is surrendered. Until tonight we have not been able to surrender, but having abandoned our homes, husbands, children and the fear of being disgraced in society, we have come to You. So what remains for us to surrender? Now please give us Your *darśana*, and by placing Your lotus feet on our heads, give us the boon of mitigating our fear of the snake of separation from You. Those feet are eternally served by Śrī Lakṣmī, so are we to be deprived of the favour of serving them because we have taken birth in cowherding families in Gokula? Those feet follow after the cows in the pastures, and You are so merciful that even without any umbrella over Your head or any shoes on Your feet You take those cows, who are merely ignorant animals, out to graze, so who could be as kind as You?" In this way, even though they were anguished, they continued to sing the glories of Kṛṣṇa's lotus feet.

In the *Bhramara-gīta*, we find the *gopīs* deriding Kṛṣṇa and accusing Him of being cruel and deceptive, but still their minds never left Him.

mṛgayur iva kapīndraṁ vivyadhe lubdha-dharmā

Śrīmad-Bhāgavatam (10.47.17)

"In Kṛṣṇa's previous life, instead of killing the innocent Vāli in the manner of a *kṣatriya*, He killed him from a hidden position like a hunter. And when a woman approached Him with amorous desires, being a *kṣatriya* He should have satisfied her; but instead, although He was excited by her beauty, He wanted to preserve

His vow to Sītā, so He made her ugly by chopping off her nose and ears. He is so eager to show that He cannot be conquered by a woman, but in that instance we can clearly see that He really had been overpowered by a woman." Even though they were accusing Kṛṣṇa, could they ever stop thinking of Him and speak about anything else?

In the verse we are discussing here, the words *tad-ālāpāḥ* mean that the *gopīs* sang in melodious tones the glories of Kṛṣṇa's names (*nāma*), qualities (*guṇa*), form (*rūpa*) and pastimes (*līlā*). This is symptomatic of *bhakti*. In the stage of *sādhana*, whenever the mind strays, it must be brought back to Bhagavān's *nāma*, *guṇa*, *rūpa* and *līlā*, and then it is real *sādhana*. There is no greater *sādhana* than this. Even endeavouring to push the thoughts of worldly enjoyment out of the mind is not necessary. The mind that has a tendency to ponder sense enjoyment should simply be engaged in hearing and describing Bhagavān's names, qualities, form and pastimes and that will be all that is necessary. Doing that more and more, then eventually these topics will become fully tasteful to us.

Tad-viceṣṭāḥ means the *gopīs* sang of Kṛṣṇa's activities that were in relation to them: how He met with them, how He fed them *tāmbūla*, how He tied bells on their ankles, how He strung garlands of flowers for them, and how when they became fatigued He wiped the dust from their faces and bodies and composed a bed of flowers for them to rest on. Then they became *tad-ātmikā* – both internally and externally they began glorifying Him, and they forgot their homes and even their very own selves. What to speak of *returning* to their homes, remembrance of the home itself didn't even arise in their minds. Glorifying Kṛṣṇa more and more in their separation, they completely forgot all worldly concerns.

Impersonalist *yogīs* don't meditate on anything; their minds become attached to the void. They don't meditate on the *ātmā*, on

Paramātmā, or on any material object either. They are *nirāśraya*, without shelter, and are therefore prone to falling down; but devotees, who follow in the footsteps of the *gopīs* and constantly meditate on Kṛṣṇa's attributes are *āśraya*, sheltered, and there is no possibility of them falling down.

Next comes this verse:

gopyas tapaḥ kim acaran yad amuṣya rūpaṁ
lāvaṇya-sāram asamordhvam ananya-siddham
dṛgbhiḥ pibanty anusavābhinavaṁ durāpam
ekānta-dhāma yaśasaḥ śriya aiśvarasya

Śrīmad-Bhāgavatam (10.44.14); *Bṛhad-bhāgavatāmṛta* (2.7.135)

[The ladies of Mathurā said:] Which austerities did the *vraja-gopīs* perform by which they could always drink through their eyes the nectar of Śrī Kṛṣṇa's form – which is the very essence of loveliness, which is unequalled or unsurpassed, which is perfect in itself and always appears new and fresh, which is extremely rare to behold and which is always the exclusive shelter of all fame, splendour and opulence?

When Kṛṣṇacandra entered the wrestling arena with Balarāma, the ladies of Mathurā spoke this verse in glorification of the *gopīs*. They said, "In this assembly, irreligious activity (*adharma*) is taking place, so we should not remain here." One should not remain in a place where sinful activities are being committed. When the attempt was made to disrobe Draupadī, that was also an assembly of *adharma*, and men of good values should not have stayed there. So why then did Grandfather Bhīṣma remain there? At that time sinful reaction did not come to him because he knew well the greatness of Bhagavān and His devotees, and he remained silent so that their greatness would be shown. He could have taken a stand against the evil men who were offending Draupadī, and he was certainly capable of killing them all single-handedly; but even though Draupadī implored him to help her, he remained silent. He was a *jñāni-bhakta*, and he knew that if someone was surrendered to Bhagavān, then He would protect them accordingly. That was his thinking, but what were those evil men thinking? "What will Bhagavān do? He has no power to stop us, so we will do as we please" and they tried to disrobe her. And what about the Pāṇḍavas? Four of them were infuriated, but Yudhiṣṭhira Mahārāja remained silent. Being a *jñāni-bhakta* also, he knew that Kṛṣṇa would protect Draupadī appropriately, but Bhīma and Arjuna, who had less awareness of Kṛṣṇa's divinity and saw Him more as a common friend in *sakhya-bhāva*, were furious.

At the wrestling arena, the ladies of Mathurā saw how those fearful wrestlers, whose massive bodies were like mountains and as if made of iron, wanted to kill soft and tender Kṛṣṇa. They saw how Baladeva's face was red with anger, and how Kṛṣṇa was smiling even though He was also angry. Considering that an injustice was about to take place, they felt that it would be shameful if they remained there. There was no one present who could prevent it: Ugrasena had been imprisoned, and other elders like Akrūra remained hidden.

The meaning of this verse is, "What austerities did the *gopīs* perform by which they could see such a beautiful and sweet form of Śrī Kṛṣṇa as He freely wandered in the forests and *kuñjas* of Vraja with a happy heart?" There the *gopīs* received the *darśana* of lovely, *rasika* Kṛṣṇa playing the flute and wearing a peacock feather in His crown. But in the wrestling arena, the ladies of Mathurā did not see that beautiful form of Kṛṣṇa; instead they saw Him in a fighting mood, after He had broken the tusks of an elephant and was decorated with drops of blood.

What is the nature of Kṛṣṇa's form? *Lāvaṇya-sāram asamordhvam* – it is the very essence of loveliness, and its beauty is unequalled and unsurpassed. Rāma is beautiful, Nārāyaṇa is beautiful and all other incarnations of Bhagavān are beautiful, but their beauty does not surpass or even equal Kṛṣṇa's beauty. *Ananya-siddham* – if Kṛṣṇa is wearing an ornament, He becomes more beautiful and if He removes that ornament, He becomes even more beautiful. Then if He becomes decorated with dust, He becomes even more beautiful again. In all circumstances He is the most beautiful; there is no necessity of His wearing any ornament such as an earring or a flower to increase His beauty. We feel a need to increase the attractiveness of our appearance – how do we appear when we are not wearing *tilaka* or when we are wearing soiled clothing? But because Kṛṣṇa has no necessity of trying to increase His beauty, He is *ananya-siddham*.

Dṛgbhiḥ pibanty anusavābhinavam – the ladies of Mathurā are saying, "That beautiful form of Śrī Kṛṣṇa which we have never seen, the *gopīs* have seen in Vraja." Suppose we have a desire to see someone whose appearance is very beautiful. Upon seeing their face just once, we become satisfied and there is no need to look again. But upon seeing Kṛṣṇa, one will have no desire to remove their gaze from Him because He always appears new and fresh. One will perpetually remain thirsty to drink the nectar of His appearance and will never desire to look away. His form is the *ekānta-dhāma* – the exclusive shelter of fame, beauty and opulence as well as the three other qualities of Bhagavān that are not mentioned in this verse. So the ladies of Mathurā are saying, "Aho! What austerities did the *gopīs* perform to receive *darśana* of that form of Śrī Kṛṣṇa? We are seeing Kṛṣṇa as He is angrily attacking His enemies, but they saw Him as the attractor of even Cupid himself."

They want to know what austerities were performed by the *gopīs* to attain *darśana* of that form, but only by aspiring to serve Kṛṣṇa in the mood of the *gopīs* can this be attained. Without an intense hankering for that, it is very, very difficult. No performance of ordinary austerities can bestow the *darśana* of that form of Kṛṣṇa that was seen by the *gopīs*. There are so many of us who chant one *lākha* of *harināma* daily, and we haven't received that *darśana* yet, so what to speak of others? There are many well-known austerities, but none of them can bestow this fruit. Some persons sit in the middle of fires in the hot season, and others bathe at four in the morning in the Yamunā in the cold season and then return home in wet cloth regardless of whether it is windy, raining, snowing, whatever. But are there any austerities by the practice of which we can attain Bhagavān?

ārādhito yadi haris tapasā tataḥ kiṁ
nārādhito yadi haristapasā tataḥ kim
antar bahir yadi haristapasā tataḥ kiṁ
nāntar bahir yadi haris tapasā tataḥ kim

Nārada-pañcarātra

What is the value of austerities performed by sages like Durvāsā if they haven't worshipped Bhagavān, and if they don't see Bhagavān everywhere? And if one *does* see Bhagavān within every living entity and everywhere outside as well, then what is the use of any other austerities besides that form of worship? For them there is no necessity of performing any austerities other than observing devotional vows like those for Ekādaśī, Janmāṣṭamī and so on. Besides chanting the holy name and hearing and meditating on *hari-kathā*, there is no method to attain Kṛṣṇa's *darśana*. The objective of performing austerities is to concentrate one's mind, but catching hold of the wind is easy in comparison to subjugating the wicked mind, so how will it be accomplished? It can only be achieved by serving Vaiṣṇavas, hearing *hari-kathā*, loudly chanting the holy name and meditating on Bhagavān.

Because the ladies of Mathurā were seeing Kṛṣṇa with *prema*, He appeared ever-new and fresh. There were others present in that arena such as the wrestlers, but did they see Him in the same way? They were not pleased upon seeing Him and instead merely became angry. Did Hiraṇyakaśipu enjoy hearing Bhagavān's name, which is sweeter than sweetness itself? So the ladies of Mathurā are saying that the *gopīs* drank the ever-fresh, enchanting form of Kṛṣṇa with their eyes just as one drinks nectar with the mouth. His form is the essence of *lāvaṇya*, loveliness. It is as if He is the very embodiment of all loveliness.

A lion that is kept in a cage does not appear very beautiful, but when it is set free in the forest, then the entirety of its beauty, power and everything are apparent. Similarly, all of Kṛṣṇa's beauty and sweetness are exhibited only "in the forest" of Vraja. He was not as beautiful in the wrestling arena with drops of the elephant's blood spattered on His face. In this connection Sanātana Gosvāmī quotes this verse from *Śrīmad-Bhāgavatam* (3.2.12):

yan-martya-līlaupayikaṁ sva-yoga-
māyā-balaṁ darśayatā gṛhītam
vismāpanaṁ svasya ca saubhagarddheḥ
paraṁ padaṁ bhūṣaṇa-bhūṣaṇāṅgam

By His Yogamāyā potency, Bhagavān Śrī Kṛṣṇa appeared in this world to lead the conditioned souls back to Him, and He exhibited a form which, upon being seen, would enchant them all. That form is the best of all, the ornament of all ornaments, and seeing it is the pinnacle of good fortune.

Chapter Sixteen

The Nature of the Gopīs' Mahābhāva

No one can taste Kṛṣṇa's beauty as the *gopīs* do. What is the reason? Only in Vraja, where Kṛṣṇa's *rūpa-mādhurī*, *līlā-mādhurī*, *veṇu-mādhurī* and *prema-mādhurī* are all present, is He overpowered by the *prema* of His associates. Of the many devotees there, none overpower Him as the *gopīs* do, and amongst them, Śrīmatī Rādhikā overpowers Him the most. Concerning this point, Sanātana Gosvāmī has written a special philosophical conclusion in his commentary to this verse. As he said before, Śrī Kṛṣṇa, the source of all incarnations, performs unlimited pastimes in unlimited *dhāmas*, but the pinnacle of His *mādhurī* flows in Vraja and nowhere else. Because the *anurāga* of the residents there is forever increasing, the entirety of His sweetness is exhibited there. Kṛṣṇa is *mādhurya*, sweet, but if the *gopīs* were not there, His sweetness would not reach its highest point. No other devotees can experience *yāvad-āśraya-vṛtti*, which is a special characteristic of the *gopīs' mahābhāva*.

To the degree that there is love for something, it can be tasted, and if there is no love, it cannot really be tasted. The meaning of *yāvad-āśraya-vṛtti* is that the *gopīs' prema* reaches as far as and even further than anyone can possibly describe it. If you stretch a rubber band it will snap at a certain point, but their *prema*, and only theirs, increases unlimitedly. Therefore they alone fully relish the *rasa* of Kṛṣṇa's four types of *mādhurī*.

The tendency to relish the unsurpassed beauty of Kṛṣṇa's form is *yāvad-āśraya-vṛtti*, another name for which is *mahābhāva*. Kṛṣṇa is *rasarāja*, and the *gopīs* are *mahābhāva*, and when they meet, the *gopīs* relish He who is the very embodiment of *rasa*. But the dynamic nature of this meeting is that sometimes Kṛṣṇa becomes *yāvad-āśraya-vṛtti*, and the *gopīs* become *rasarāja*. This is not possible for anyone else but the *gopīs*; being overpowered by their *prema*, Kṛṣṇa begins serving and attending them.

Suppose there is a young boy who is lame, ugly and unable to speak properly. It is doubtful that others will be very affectionate towards him, but his mother will always love him. Why? Because she possesses *anurāga*, spontaneous love for him, and although that is simply a reflection of the genuine sentiment, *anurāga* is the root cause of love. Because the *gopīs' anurāga* for Kṛṣṇa expands unlimitedly, it is called *yāvad-āśraya-vṛtti*. Upon receiving Kṛṣṇa's *darśana*, the *gopīs'* love multiplies millions of times – this is the *vṛtti*, tendency, of their *anurāga*. But this only occurs when they see the unsurpassed *mādhurya* of *Kṛṣṇa's* form; it does not happen when they see anyone else, including Uddhava, who looks so much like Kṛṣṇa.

The ladies of Mathurā lamented that although they were seeing Kṛṣṇa directly, they did not possess the quality of *prema* for Him by which they could see His form of unsurpassed beauty as the *gopīs* always did. A person eats something with great pleasure when they are hungry. And if someone isn't hungry, they may pinch a bit of the preparation off with their nails, examine it, find fault with it and not desire to eat it. But if one is hungry, he will consider any preparation to be tasteful, even if it is stale. Then what to speak of that preparation which is unlimitedly sweet? In this way, the *gopīs'* "hunger" for Kṛṣṇa is such that as they taste Kṛṣṇa's *mādhurya*, their *mahābhāva* increases so much that it knows no upper limit. Even though there is no space for it to increase any further, still it increases. In the upper stages of *mahābhāva* known as *mādana* and *modana*, it perpetually increases and feels ever-new and fresh.

In our present condition we cannot estimate even a fraction of that, but when our faith in the spiritual master, the Vaiṣṇavas and Bhagavān is sufficiently developed, then as we become free from the influence of our *anarthas*, *niṣṭhā* will come. Even if we possess some *śraddhā* and *niṣṭhā* in partial form, still, our *ruci* must become deep. For now our minds may not remain steady, but someday *bhāva* will come to us, and precisely when it will come is not in our hands. It is solely in the hands of Bhagavān and those devotees who possess that *bhāva*, and only when they bestow their mercy will it come to us. At that time even the experience of *mahābhāva* will come to a deserving soul automatically, even though he may have not previously known anything of that tendency. It may seem that there is no hope of it ever coming and no space whatsoever for it in our hearts, but still it will come automatically. Then by its wonderful influence one will easily cross over whatever seemingly insurmountable obstacles may exist in this world.

The ladies of Mathurā speak of *mādhurya* Kṛṣṇa who had come to Mathurā from Vraja. Why didn't He bring His flute with Him to Mathurā? Because if He were to play the flute in Mathurā, no lady would leave her home and family in the dead of night to come to Him; there was no qualified recipient for the flute-song in Mathurā. The ladies there saw His beautiful form, but would they ever leave their husbands to go to Him? Would it happen in Dvārakā? All would be afraid of transgressing their *dharma* and being disgraced in society. Because *mahābhāva* and *yāvad-āśraya-vṛtti* do not exist there, no one would come.

In this regard Sanātana Gosvāmī says in his commentary that a devotee will perform *kīrtana* and hear *hari-kathā* of his worshipful deity, but direct experience of Him will only come in the *dhāma*. A devotee may meditate on Kṛṣṇa, become absorbed in remembrance of Him, and gain some attachment for the *bhāva* of Vraja, but direct experience of Kṛṣṇa can come only in Vṛndāvana, whether it is Gokula or Goloka. In other places meditation and remembrance are possible, but direct experience of Him is available only in Vṛndāvana. Therefore Kṛṣṇa's eternal associates in Dvārakā and Mathurā may also be able to estimate the *mādhurya* of Kṛṣṇa in Vraja to a certain degree, but could they ever achieve direct experience of it? Would they ever be able to abandon everything and come to Kṛṣṇa in the dead of night? No, and neither would Kṛṣṇa ever enter the royal assembly hall in Dvārakā in His Vraja attire.

Mahābhāva is unlimitedly variegated. Ordinarily it is said that *mahābhāva* is of two varieties, *rūḍha* and *adhirūḍha*, but thousands of variations of each of them are possible, some in meeting and some in separation. But all varieties of *mahābhāva* are embodied in Śrīmatī Rādhikā, or they are manifest in Her expansions as the *sakhīs*. She is the *svayaṁ-rūpa* of *mahābhāva*, as Kṛṣṇa is the *svayaṁ-rūpā* and source of the *tad-ekātma*, *svāṁśaka*, *vilāsa*, *āveśa*, *prābhava-prakāśa*, *vaibhava-prakāśa* and *guṇa* expansions. The *guṇa-avatāras* are Brahmā, Viṣṇu and Śaṅkara, and the *āveśa-avatāras* include Pṛthu, Nārada, Vyāsa, Kapila and Paraśurāma. They all possess specific natures or empowerments. Then when Kṛṣṇa expands into forms that are fully *sac-cid-ānanda* and *sarva-śaktimān*, it is called *tad-ekātma-rūpa*.

As all these personalities expand from Him and perpetually exist within Him, Rādhā embodies all of the three hundred and sixty varieties of heroines. Due to this She always attracts Kṛṣṇa's mind. If Kṛṣṇa desires a specific *bhāva,* and in one *gopī* it is found to be insufficient, He can attain it by associating with another *gopī*. But none of them can completely mystify and enchant Him as only Rādhikā can.

Because unlimited feelings and desires arise within Kṛṣṇa, as the best lover and the hero of all women He is sometimes *dhīrodātta* (grave and gentle), sometimes *dhīra-śanta* (peaceful and forbearing), sometimes *dhīra-lalita* (carefree and jovial) and sometimes *dhīroddhata* (proud and restless). He is all of these at the same time, and when there is the necessity for only one of these moods, He manifests that specific one. In the same way, Śrīmatī Rādhikā manifests whatever mood is necessary, sometimes becoming *dhīra* (grave), sometimes *māninī* (pouting) and sometimes *dakṣiṇa* (clever). As the crown jewel and very embodiment of the three hundred and sixty varieties of heroines, She relishes the sweetness of Kṛṣṇa to the utmost. Because She can manifest all the qualities of all the varieties of heroines, She is known as *mādanākhya-bhāva-vatī*.

While meeting with Kṛṣṇa She experiences *mādana*, and in separation from Him She experiences *mohana*. Śrī Caitanya Mahāprabhu showed something of these elevated states of Hers to the world, and besides Him there has never been anyone in this world who could exhibit these things. However, when He was exhibiting these states, Rāya Rāmānanda and Svarūpa Dāmodara, due to being His intimate associates, could also relish something of them. Besides them no one else could comprehend these sentiments, but later Mahāprabhu invested the potency to understand them directly into the heart of Rūpa Gosvāmī, saying, "He will manifest My *bhāva* in this world through his writings."

As Rādhikā experiences unlimited pastimes, the twenty varieties of ecstatic symptoms beginning with *kila-kiñcita* arise in Her simultaneously. She Herself cannot comprehend all these sentiments, and the appropriate sentiment is always manifest in Her at the correct time for Kṛṣṇa's pleasure. Because of this, She is eternally the beloved of Kṛṣṇa in His *svayaṁ-rūpa*. He never appears to Her as any *kāya-vyūha* expansion, or simply by *sphūrti* (arising in Her meditation), but is always with Her in His original form – in both meeting and separation.

Once, Rādhikā was seated somewhere in Vraja meditating on Kṛṣṇa more and more until She suddenly became completely overwhelmed. Then from behind someone placed their hands over Her eyes. She called out, "Lalitā?" But the hands were not removed; only when She called out the name of the person covering Her eyes would the hands be removed. "Viśākhā? Citrā? Kundalatā?" She called out the names of all Her *sakhīs*, but still the hands were not removed. When She said, "Śyāmasundara!" then He removed His hands and joyfully sat beside Her. Sanātana Gosvāmī comments on this pastime that Rādhikā thought that Kṛṣṇa appeared by *sphūrti* – in Her meditation, or that because at that time He was present in Mathurā or Dvārakā in His original form, He must have come there by assuming a *kāya-vyūha* expansion. But he concludes that Kṛṣṇa must have appeared there in His *svayaṁ-rūpa*, because otherwise Rādhikā would not be fully satisfied. This is the wonderful conception of Sanātana Gosvāmī.

If Mahāprabhu is in Purī, but in Navadvīpa Mother Śacī is crying while making an offering to Him, would she be satisfied if He were to appear there in a mere *kāya-vyūha* expansion? Knowing that she would only be satisfied if He came in His original form, He does just that, and it is the same with Śrīmatī Rādhikā. In His original form Kṛṣṇa always remains by the side of Rādhikā, and is never able to be separated from Her. Sanātana Gosvāmī says that because the *vraja-devīs* possess the paramount *mahābhāva* – *yāvad-āśraya-vṛtti* – how could Kṛṣṇa ever leave them? Even while residing in a foreign land He visits them in Vṛndāvana in His original form – and only them, not others such as the *sakhās*.

rākhite tomāra jīvana, sevi āmi nārāyaṇa,
tāṅra śaktye āsi niti-niti
tomā-sane krīḍā kari', niti yāi yadu-purī,
tāhā tumi mānaha mora sphūrti

mora bhāgya mo-vasaye, tomāra ye prema haye,
sei prema-parama prabala
lukāñā āmā āne, saṅga karāya tomā-sane,
prakaṭeha ānibe satvara

Śrī Caitanya-caritāmṛta (*Madhya-līlā* 13.154–5)

Sitting alone with Rādhā in Vraja, Kṛṣṇa says, "My dearest Śrīmatī Rādhikā, in the distant land of Dvārakā I have married many ladies, but in reality I don't love any of them as I love You. I searched the entire universe for one *kiśorī* whose beauty, complexion and nature was like Yours. I found Satyabhāmā, but I remain with her only because she reminds Me of You; and similarly I have married sixteen thousand queens because each of them reminds Me of the *gopīs*. If somehow that remembrance of You were to be lost, I would leave them all at once. You say that when we are apart You feel as if You are dying, but I am constantly meditating on how to save Your life, and for this purpose I worship Nārāyaṇa. By His mercy and mystical potency, I am able to come to Vṛndāvana every day to enjoy Your company. You consider My appearance to be in Your meditation or in a *kāya-vyūha* form but I come to Vṛndāvana in My original form. My great good fortune is the immense love that You have for Me. Unknown to everyone in Dvārakā and in Vṛndāvana, I come here to You, and hopefully very soon I will also be visible to everyone else here."

In the verse we are discussing are the words *amuṣya rūpam*, meaning "that very form". The ladies of Mathurā are saying, "We are seeing Kṛṣṇa, but why are we not feeling the highest *prema*? What austerities did the *gopīs* perform to be able to see with the eyes of *mahābhāva* the original form of Kṛṣṇa – adorned with a peacock feather in His crown, and as the very essence of all loveliness?" Unable to see that form of Kṛṣṇa that the *gopīs* see and unable to experience the *mahābhāva* of the *gopīs*, they wanted to know which austerities they could perform to become similarly fortunate.

Not everyone will be able to feel such elevated *bhāva*. When our *gurudeva*, Śrīla Bhakti Prajñāna Keśava Gosvāmī Mahārāja, would dance, he would move in an exceptionally sweet and lovely way. With his eyes turned upwards and holding his *sannyāsa-daṇḍa* in his hand, he would dance immersed in *bhāva*. I have never seen such dancing as his in all my life. Whenever he would hear Kṛṣṇa's pastimes he would become emotional and begin weeping, and if we perform *bhajana* sincerely with resolute determination, we may also one day experience some of this *bhāva*. We desire these feelings as do the ladies of Mathurā who lamented, "*Hāya! Hāya!* We are seeing Kṛṣṇa directly, yet we cannot experience the *bhāva* of the *gopīs*. Our lives are useless!"

Sanātana Gosvāmī says that only in Vraja can the sweet form of Kṛṣṇa as the essence of loveliness and the emporium of *rasa* be seen, and only in Vraja can such a sweet *bhāva* be experienced. Outside Vraja, Kṛṣṇa's original form cannot be seen directly, and this *bhāva* cannot be directly relished. In other places one may possibly see Kṛṣṇa by meditation or in one of His expansions, but direct experience of Him is not possible.

Next comes this verse:

yā dohane 'vahanane mathanopalepa-
preṅkheṅkhanārbha-ruditokṣaṇa-mārjanādau
gāyanti cainam anurakta-dhiyo 'śru-kaṇṭhyo
dhanyā vraja-striya urukrama-citta-yānāḥ

Śrīmad-Bhāgavatam (10.44.15); *Bṛhad-bhāgavatāmṛta* (2.7.136)

The *gopīs* are extremely fortunate, because their hearts are always so absorbed in Śrī Kṛṣṇa that while milking cows, churning yoghurt, applying *candana* and other decorations to their bodies, comforting crying babies, washing their floors and performing all other household duties, tears of love flow from their eyes as they continuously sing about His purifying fame.

Generally, when a *kaniṣṭha-adhikārī* goes to visit a *mahā-bhāgavata* Vaiṣṇava, he first thinks "He is a *kaniṣṭha-adhikārī* just like me." At first, Sarvabhauma Bhaṭṭācārya ridiculed Rāya Rāmānanda, thinking that he spoke too highly about women – Sarvabhauma considered the *gopīs* to be ordinary women. He only respected the scholarship of the four Kumāras, the renunciation of Śukadeva Gosvāmī and the impersonal conception of Śaṅkarācārya. Therefore if one isn't of a higher type himself, he won't be able to understand the *bhāva* of higher devotees. And only a great, perfected personality who is *rāgātmikā*, a devotee who is in the final stage of *rāgānuga-sādhana*, will understand the *prema* of the *gopīs*. Even devotees such as Bhīṣma who were contemporary with them could not fully understand the exalted nature of their *prema*. Only those who were near them could understand something of it. For instance, Uddhava had to leave Dvārakā and go to Vraja to understand something about how exalted the *gopīs* were; if he had remained in Dvārakā, he would have never understood.

This verse and the previous one were spoken by the ladies of Mathurā, and because Mathurā is only five miles from Vraja, sometimes the spiritual greed of the devotees of Vraja would find its way to Mathurā. Besides Uddhava, sometimes tradesmen and others would travel back and forth between Vraja and Mathurā, and in this way the residents of Mathurā would be able to understand something of the *bhāva* of Vraja; but those who lived far away from Vraja understood nothing of it.

Even in separation from Kṛṣṇa, the *gopīs* were always meeting Him. While looking after their children, milking the cows, churning yoghurt, applying *candana* and doing housework, they always received His direct *darśana* through singing about Him, and therefore *kīrtana* is the best devotional activity. Singing in unison in a soft morning *rāga*, they saw Kṛṣṇa with the eyes of *bhāva*, even though not abandoning their duties. Similarly, a *sādhaka* will observe all the rules and regulations of *vaidhī-bhakti*, but internally his *bhāva* should be of *rāgānuga-bhakti*. Externally he will appear to be the same, but internally his *bhāva* will be different. The greed of *rāgānugā* will take one to Vraja, whereas *vaidhī-bhakti* will take one only to Vaikuṇṭha. Because the ladies of Mathurā are in close proximity to Vraja and therefore the *bhāva* of Vraja, they are praying that they will also experience the *bhāva* of the *gopīs*.

At the time of the *rāsa-līlā*, Kṛṣṇa and the *gopīs* were singing together. In beautiful melodies saturated with *rasa*, the *gopīs* defeated Kṛṣṇa by singing "*Kṛṣṇa sādhu, Kṛṣṇa sādhu*" in a note higher than Kṛṣṇa could sing. As the ladies of Mathurā contemplated pastimes such as this which the *gopīs* enjoyed with Kṛṣṇa, they said, "Whereas we can only see Kṛṣṇa here in a fighting mood, the *gopīs* perpetually see Him in His form as the crown jewel of *vidagdha*. We have never received such good fortune!" *Vidagdha* means witty and ingenious, but when applied to Kṛṣṇa it means He who is *rasika-catura* – supremely clever and skilful in relishing *rasa*. These ladies of Mathurā were not even as fortunate as the Pulinda girl, who often heard the vibration of Kṛṣṇa's flute. Even the deer of Vraja heard the melody of His flute, but the ladies of Mathurā could only imagine it.

All of our duties should be performed while singing *nāma-saṅkīrtana*. Suppose there is a pitcher of water. If we simply add some lemon juice and some sugar, it immediately becomes nectar. Similarly, we must perform so many worldly duties, but if, following in the *bhāva* of our spiritual master, we meditate on Bhagavān while carrying them out, they will all become nectar. In the conditioned state, we are always considering what is favourable and what is unfavourable to our *bhakti*. Because we are in the beginning stages, everything appears to be unfavourable to us, and therefore our minds are disturbed. But to the degree which we progress in *sādhana-bhajana* means to that degree the vision of what is unfavourable will diminish. And when one reaches the stage of *bhāva*, he will perceive everything that he previously considered to be unfavourable as favourable.

Actually, nothing in this world is unfavourable to us; it is only due to our present weaknesses and *anarthas* that we see our environment as unfavourable. Whatever obstacles we are currently facing are due to our own previous misdeeds, and are not the fault of any other person.

In this verse, the *rasika* ladies of Mathurā say *urukrama-citta-yānāḥ*: the *gopīs'* minds flow spontaneously towards Urukrama-Kṛṣṇa. *Uru* means a strong, continuous current, and because their minds spontaneously flow towards Kṛṣṇa with great speed and force, they are fortunate, and thus Kṛṣṇa comes to them directly while they are singing. So if while carrying out our household duties our minds and hearts are absorbed in Kṛṣṇa's *nāma*, *rūpa*, *guṇa* and *līlā*, then very soon we will receive His direct *darśana*.

Bhakti-rasāyana verses

dhanyeyam adya dharaṇī tṛṇa-vīrudhas tvat-
pāda-spṛśo druma-latāḥ karajābhimṛṣṭāḥ
nadyo 'drayaḥ khaga-mṛgāḥ sadayāvalokair
gopyo 'ntareṇa bhujayor api yat-spṛhā śrīḥ

Śrīmad-Bhāgavatam (10.15.8); *Bṛhad-bhāgavatāmṛta* (2.7.107)

[Śrī Kṛṣṇa said to Balarāma:] Today this land, along with all its green grass, has become fortunate due to receiving the touch of your lotus feet. And receiving the touch of the fingers of your lotus hands, the trees, creepers and bushes consider that they have attained the greatest treasure. Receiving your affectionate glances, the rivers, mountains, birds and animals are all feeling fully gratified. But most fortunate of all are the *vraja-gopīs*, who have been embraced to Your strong chest, a favour which even Lakṣmī-devī herself always desires.

vṛndāvanaṁ sakhi bhuvo vitanoti kīrtiṁ
yad devakī-suta-padāmbuja-labdha-lakṣmi
govinda-veṇum anu matta-mayūra-nṛtyam
prekṣyādri-sānv-avaratānya-samasta-sattvam

Śrīmad-Bhāgavatam (10.21.10); *Bṛhad-bhāgavatāmṛta* (2.7.108)

[The *gopīs* said:] O *sakhī*, this Vṛndāvana is expanding the glories of the Earth planet because it is being adorned with the lotus footprints of Śrī Kṛṣṇa. Hearing Him play a soft and deep note on the flute, the peacocks have become maddened and have begun dancing. Beholding this spectacle, all of the birds and animals who reside on the mountainside have abandoned their usual restive activities.

hantāyam adrir abalā hari-dāsa-varyo
yad-rāma-kṛṣṇa-caraṇa-sparaśa-pramodaḥ
mānaṁ tanoti saha-go-gaṇayos tayor yat
pānīya-sūyavasa-kandara-kandamūlaiḥ

Śrīmad-Bhāgavatam (10.21.18); *Bṛhad-bhāgavatāmṛta* (2.7.109)

[The *gopīs* said:] This Govardhana Hill is the best of all those who are known as *hari-dāsa* because he is feeling great jubilation from the touch of the lotus feet of Kṛṣṇa and Balarāma. With great respect Govardhana is worshipping them by providing all their necessities such as caves, fruits, flowers and water for their pleasure, and for the pleasure of their cowherd friends, cows and calves.

dṛṣṭvātape vraja-paśūn saha rāma-gopaiḥ
sañcārayantam anu veṇum udīrayantam
prema-pravṛddha uditaḥ kusumāvalībhiḥ
sakhyur vyadhāt sva-vapuṣāmbuda ātapatram

Śrīmad-Bhāgavatam (10.21.16); *Bṛhad-bhāgavatāmṛta* (2.7.110)

[The *gopīs* said:] Seeing Kṛṣṇa and Balarāma playing their flutes in the afternoon sun and taking the cows and calves out for grazing, the clouds burst with divine love, and like an umbrella shield their friend Śrī Kṛṣṇa from the sun while showering tiny drops of rain that are like a shower of flowers." (Kṛṣṇa has been referred to here as a friend of the clouds because their natures are similar. Both are dark blue in complexion, and as Kṛṣṇa eradicates the heat of material existence by bestowing the nectar of His mercy, the clouds give relief from the heat of this world by showering rain. Kṛṣṇa also plays soft and deep melodies on His flute that resemble the clouds' thunder.)

nadyas tadā tad upadhārya mukunda-gītam
āvarta-lakṣita-manobhava-bhagna-vegāḥ
āliṅgana-sthagitam ūrmi-bhujair murārer
gṛhṇanti pāda-yugalaṁ kamalopahārāḥ

Śrīmad-Bhāgavatam (10.21.15); *Bṛhad-bhāgavatāmṛta* (2.7.111)

[The *gopīs* said:] O *sakhīs*, when the rivers of Vṛndāvana headed by the Yamunā hear the vibration of Kṛṣṇa's flute, their currents completely stop, and their waters begin to swirl as if they are overcome with desire. With their arms in the form of waves they reach out to touch and offer lotus flowers to His lotus feet.

vana-latās tarava ātmani viṣṇuṁ
vyañjayantya iva puṣpa-phalāḍhyāḥ
praṇata-bhāra-viṭapā madhu-dhārāḥ
prema-hṛṣṭa-tanavo vavṛṣuḥ sma

Śrīmad-Bhāgavatam (10.35.9); *Bṛhad-bhāgavatāmṛta* (2.7.112)

[The *gopīs* said:] Look how the creepers and the branches of the trees of Vṛndāvana are drooping down due to their weight! They must have also taken Śrī Kṛṣṇa within their hearts, because tears of love in the form of streams of honey are dripping from them, and the emergence of their fruits and flowers bear witness to their ecstatic rapture.

ete 'linas tava yaśo 'khila-loka-tīrthaṁ
gāyanta ādi-puruṣānupathaṁ bhajante
prāyo amī muni-gaṇā bhavadīya-mukhyā
gūḍhaṁ vane 'pi na jahaty anaghātma-daivam

Śrīmad-Bhāgavatam (10.15.6); *Bṛhad-bhāgavatāmṛta* (2.7.113)

[Śrī Kṛṣṇa said to Balarāma:] O Ādi-puruṣa, although you are keeping your opulences hidden and are performing pastimes as a young boy here in Vṛndāvana, still the *munis*, who are among the best of your devotees, have recognised you. Not wanting to be separated from you for even one moment, they have assumed the forms of bees and are worshipping you by constantly singing your glories as the purifier of this world.

sarasi sārasa-haṁsa-vihaṅgāś
cāru-gīta-hṛta-cetasa etya
harim upāsata te yata-cittā
hanta-mīlita-dṛśo dhṛta-maunāḥ

Śrīmad-Bhāgavatam (10.35.11); *Bṛhad-bhāgavatāmṛta* (2.7.114)

[The *gopīs* said:] It is very astonishing that Kṛṣṇa steals away the hearts of the swans, cranes and other water-birds in such a way that they approach Him, sit down and worship Him with their eyes closed, and fully concentrate their minds on Him.

prāyo batāmba vihagā munayo vane 'smin
kṛṣṇekṣitaṁ tad-uditaṁ kala-veṇu-gītam
āruhya ye druma-bhujān rucira-pravālān
śṛṇvanti mīlita-dṛśo vigatānya-vācaḥ

Śrīmad-Bhāgavatam (10.21.14); *Bṛhad-bhāgavatāmṛta* (2.7.115)

[The *gopīs* said:] O friend, the birds of Vṛndāvana are actually sages. They have taken positions on the branches of trees that have new and fresh leaves from where they can easily have *darśana* of Śrī Kṛṣṇa. Sitting there and hearing the sweet vibration of His flute, they close their eyes and become immersed in divine bliss.

dhanyāḥ sma mūḍha-gatayo 'pi hariṇya etā
yā nanda-nandanam upātta-vicitra-veśam
ākarṇya veṇu-raṇitaṁ saha-kṛṣṇa-sārāḥ
pūjāṁ dadhur viracitāṁ praṇayāvalokaiḥ

Śrīmad-Bhāgavatam (10.21.11); *Bṛhad-bhāgavatāmṛta* (2.7.116)

[The *gopīs* said:] These ignorant deer are also fortunate, because accompanied by their husbands they are standing motionlessly and listening to the vibration of Kṛṣṇa's flute. It is as if they are offering *pūjā* to the gorgeously attired son of Nanda with their loving glances.

gāvaś ca kṛṣṇa-mukha-nirgata-veṇu-gīta-
pīyūṣam uttabhita-karṇa-puṭaiḥ pibantyaḥ
śāvāḥ snuta-stana-payaḥ-kavalāḥ sma tasthur
govindam ātmani dṛśāśru-kalāḥ spṛśantyaḥ

Śrīmad-Bhāgavatam (10.21.13); *Bṛhad-bhāgavatāmṛta* (2.7.117)

[The *gopīs* said:] In order to drink the nectarean vibration of the flute-song emanating from the lotus mouth of Śrī Kṛṣṇa, the cows have raised their ears. The grass which they were chewing just remains in their mouths, and milk begins to drip from their udders. The calves at once stop drinking their mothers' milk, and as they embrace Kṛṣṇa within their hearts, tears of love begin to glide down their faces.

vṛndaśo vraja-vṛṣā mṛga-gāvo
veṇu-vādya-hṛta-cetasa ārāt
danta-daṣṭa-kavalā dhṛta-karṇā
nidritā likhita-citram ivāsan

Śrīmad-Bhāgavatam (10.35.5); *Bṛhad-bhāgavatāmṛta* (2.7.118)

[The *gopīs* said:] Hearing the vibration of Śrī Kṛṣṇa's flute, the bulls, cows and deer of Vṛndāvana approach Him. Unable to swallow the grass that they had taken into their mouths, they stand silently with their ears raised and appear like animals in a painting.

pūrṇāḥ pulindya urugāya-padābja-rāga-
śrī-kuṅkumena dayitā-stana-maṇḍitena
tad-darśana-smara-rujas tṛṇa-rūṣitena
limpantya ānana-kuceṣu jahus tad-ādhim

Śrīmad-Bhāgavatam (10.21.17); *Bṛhad-bhāgavatāmṛta* (2.7.119)

[The *gopīs* said:] O *sakhī*, we consider the Pulinda girls who collect grass and wood to be greatly fortunate, because by spreading the *kuṅkuma* that lies upon the grass on their faces and bodies, the desires which arise in their hearts from seeing that very *kuṅkuma* are pacified. In reality, that *kuṅkuma* is from the breasts of Śrīmatī Rādhikā, and at the time of enjoying pastimes with Śrī Kṛṣṇa, it becomes smeared on His lotus feet. Then as They wander in the forest, it falls from His feet onto the grass.

yadi dūraṁ gataḥ kṛṣṇo
vana-śobhekṣaṇāya tam
ahaṁ pūrvam ahaṁ pūrvam
iti saṁspṛśya remire

Śrīmad-Bhāgavatam (10.12.6); *Bṛhad-bhāgavatāmṛta* (2.7.120)

[Śrī Śukadeva Gosvāmī said:] When Śrī Kṛṣṇa would sometimes wander far away to see the splendour of the forest, the cowherd boys would revel in running after Him, saying, "I will be the first to touch Him! I will be the first to touch Him!"

itthaṁ satāṁ brahma-sukhānubhūtyā
dāsyaṁ gatānāṁ para-daivatena
māyāśritānāṁ nara-dārakeṇa
sārdhaṁ vijahruḥ kṛta-puṇya-puñjāḥ

Śrīmad-Bhāgavatam (10.12.11); *Bṛhad-bhāgavatāmṛta* (2.7.121)

[Śrī Śukadeva Gosvāmī said:] In this way the greatly fortunate cowherd boys enjoy in various ways with Śrī Kṛṣṇa, who is seen as the Brahman effulgence by the *jñānīs*, as the supremely worshipful deity by His servants and as an ordinary boy by people in general. (Or *māyāśrita* can also mean that those who had received His utmost mercy, due to being devoid of the mood of opulence, saw Him merely as the son of Nanda.)

yat-pāda-pāṁśur bahu-janma-kṛcchrato
dhṛtātmabhir yogibhir apy alābhyaḥ
sa eva yād-dṛg viṣayaḥ svayaṁ sthitaḥ
kiṁ varṇyate diṣṭam aho vrajaukasām

Śrīmad-Bhāgavatam (10.12.12); *Bṛhad-bhāgavatāmṛta* (2.7.122)

[Śrī Śukadeva Gosvāmī said:] Great *yogīs* perform severe austerities for many lifetimes, but even when with great difficulty they have completely controlled their minds, they still cannot attain even one particle of the dust of the lotus feet of Śrī Kṛṣṇa. How then can I possibly describe the good fortune of the Vrajavāsīs, who daily received His direct *darśana*?

kvacit pallava-talpeṣu
niyuddha-śrama-karśitaḥ
vṛkṣa-mūlāśrayaḥ śete
gopotsaṅgopabarhaṇaḥ

Śrīmad-Bhāgavatam (10.15.16); *Bṛhad-bhāgavatāmṛta* (2.7.123)

[Śrī Śukadeva Gosvāmī said:] When Śrī Kṛṣṇa would become fatigued from wrestling with the cowherd boys, He would accept the lap of one of His friends as a pillow and lie down beneath a tree on a richly decorated bed of flowers and leaves.

pāda-saṁvāhanaṁ cakruḥ
kecit tasya mahātmanaḥ
apare hata-pāpmāno
vyajanaiḥ samavījayan

Śrīmad-Bhāgavatam (10.15.17); *Bṛhad-bhāgavatāmṛta* (2.7.124)

[Śrī Śukadeva Gosvāmī said:] At that time, one greatly fortunate *sakhā* would massage His feet, and another would fan His body with a fan made of leaves.

anye tad-anurūpāṇi
manojñāni mahātmanaḥ
gāyanti sma mahā-rāja
sneha-klinna-dhiyaḥ śanaiḥ

Śrīmad-Bhāgavatam (10.15.18); *Bṛhad-bhāgavatāmṛta* (2.7.125)

[Śrī Śukadeva Gosvāmī said:] My dear Mahārāja, other *sakhās* would sing attractive songs appropriate for resting-time, and all the cowherd boys' hearts would melt in affection for Kṛṣṇa.

nandaḥ kim akarod brāhman
śreya evaṁ mahodayam
yaśodā vā mahā-bhāgā
papau yasyāḥ stanaṁ hariḥ

Śrīmad-Bhāgavatam (10.8.46); *Bṛhad-bhāgavatāmṛta* (2.7.126)

[Śrī Parīkṣit Mahārāja asked:] My dear *brāhmaṇa*, which supremely auspicious *sādhana* did Nanda perform, and which austerities did the supremely fortunate Yaśodā undergo to have her breast-milk drunk by Śrī Hari?

tato bhaktir bhagavati
putrī-bhūte janārdane
dampatyor nitarām āsīd
gopa-gopīṣu bhārata

Śrīmad-Bhāgavatam (10.8.51); *Bṛhad-bhāgavatāmṛta* (2.7.127)

[Śrī Śukadeva Gosvāmī replied:] O Bharata, for fulfilling the promise of His dear devotee Brahmā, Śrī Kṛṣṇa, the Supreme Lord Himself and the destroyer of evil, appeared as the son of Nanda and Yaśodā. In comparison to all of the other *gopas* and *gopīs*, this couple possessed the most love for Him.

nandaḥ sva-putram ādāya
proṣyāgatam udāra-dhīḥ
mūrdhny avaghrāya paramaṁ
mudaṁ lebhe kurūdvaha

Śrīmad-Bhāgavatam (10.6.43); *Bṛhad-bhāgavatāmṛta* (2.7.128)

[Śrī Śukadeva Gosvāmī said:] When magnanimous Nanda returned from Mathurā, he took his own son Śrī Kṛṣṇa on his lap and experienced immense pleasure by repeatedly smelling His head.

sa mātuḥ svinna-gātrāya
visrasta-kavara-srajaḥ
dṛṣṭvā pariśramaṁ kṛṣṇaḥ
kṛpayāsīt sva-bandhane

Śrīmad-Bhāgavatam (10.9.18); *Bṛhad-bhāgavatāmṛta* (2.7.129)

[Śrī Śukadeva Gosvāmī said:] When Kṛṣṇa saw Yaśodā labouring so desperately that her whole body was dripping with perspiration and the flower garland that was entwined in her hair braid was falling down, He mercifully allowed Himself to be bound by her.

nemaṁ viriñco na bhavo
na śrīr apy aṅga-saṁśrayā
prasādaṁ lebhire gopī
yat tat prāpa vimuktidāt

Śrīmad-Bhāgavatam (10.9.20); *Bṛhad-bhāgavatāmṛta* (2.7.130)

[Śrī Śukadeva Gosvāmī said:] Neither Brahmā, Śiva, or even Lakṣmī-devī – who eternally resides at Kṛṣṇa's chest in the form of a golden line – have ever received as much mercy as Yaśodā did from He who is the bestower of liberation.

payaṁsi yāsām apibat
putra-sneha-snutāny alam
bhagavān devakī-putraḥ
kaivalyādy-akhilārtha-daḥ

Śrīmad-Bhāgavatam (10.6.39); *Bṛhad-bhāgavatāmṛta* (2.7.131)

[Śrī Śukadeva Gosvāmī said:] Bhagavān Śrī Kṛṣṇa, the bestower of all the objectives of human pursuit including all varieties of liberation, drank with full satisfaction the milk of all the motherly *gopīs* and cows who were dripping with milk due to their motherly affection for Him.

tāsām aviratam kṛṣṇe
kurvatīnāṁ suteksaṇam
na punaḥ kalpate rājan
saṁsāro 'jñāna-sambhavaḥ

Śrīmad-Bhāgavatam (10.6.40); *Bṛhad-bhāgavatāmṛta* (2.7.132)

[Śrī Śukadeva Gosvāmī said:] O King, those *gopīs* and cows were always feeling maternal love for Kṛṣṇa, and therefore after leaving their bodies they could have never re-entered the cycle of birth and death, the calamity which is imposed on those who are ignorant.

gopīnāṁ paramānanda
āsīd govinda-darśane
kṣaṇaṁ yuga-śatam iva
yāsāṁ yena vinābhavat

Śrīmad-Bhāgavatam (10.19.16); *Bṛhad-bhāgavatāmṛta* (2.7.133)

[Śrī Śukadeva Gosvāmī said:] The *vraja-gopīs* would experience supreme pleasure upon receiving the *darśana* of Śrī Govinda, but they would consider one moment of His absence to be like one hundred *yugas*.

tan-manaskās tad-ālāpās
tad-viceṣṭās tad-ātmikāḥ
tad-guṇān eva gāyantyo
nātmāgārāṇi sasmaruḥ

Śrīmad-Bhāgavatam (10.30.43); *Bṛhad-bhāgavatāmṛta* (2.7.134)

[Śrī Śukadeva Gosvāmī said:] Those *vraja-gopīs*, who had fully given their hearts to Śrī Kṛṣṇa, would imitate His manner of speaking and His activities. Since they had offered their very souls to Him and always sang His glories, they completely forgot themselves and their family interests.

gopyas tapaḥ kim acaran yad amuṣya rūpaṁ
lāvaṇya-sāram asamordhvam ananya-siddham
dṛgbhiḥ pibanty anusavābhinavaṁ durāpam
ekānta-dhāma yaśasaḥ śriya aiśvarasya

Śrīmad-Bhāgavatam (10.44.14); *Bṛhad-bhāgavatāmṛta* (2.7.135)

[The ladies of Mathurā said:] Which austerities did the *vraja-gopīs* perform by which they could always drink through their eyes the nectar of Śrī Kṛṣṇa's form – which is the very essence of loveliness, which is unequalled or unsurpassed, which is perfect in itself and always appears new and fresh, which is extremely rare to behold and which is always the exclusive shelter of all fame, splendour and opulence?

yā dohane 'vahanane mathanopalepa-
preṅkheṅkhanārbha-ruditokṣaṇa-mārjanādau
gāyanti cainam anurakta-dhiyo 'śru-kaṇṭhyo
dhanyā vraja-striya urukrama-citta-yānāḥ

Śrīmad-Bhāgavatam (10.44.15); *Bṛhad-bhāgavatāmṛta* (2.7.136)

[The ladies of Mathurā said:] The *gopīs* are extremely fortunate, because their hearts are always so absorbed in Śrī Kṛṣṇa that while milking cows, churning yoghurt, applying *candana* and other decorations to their bodies, comforting crying babies, washing their floors and performing all other household duties, tears of love flow from their eyes as they continuously sing about His purifying fame.

Glossary

A

ācārya – spiritual preceptor; one who teaches by example.

adhirūḍha – the highest state of *mahābhāva*, found only in the *gopīs* of Vraja. The mood in which all the *anubhāvas* that are manifested in resolute *mahābhāva* attain special characteristics that are even more astonishing than those *anubhāvas* in their normal forms.

anarthas – unwanted desires in the heart, which impede one's advancement in devotional life.

añjana – an ointment used to darken the edges of the eyelids.

arcana – deity worship; one of the nine primary processes of devotional service.

anurāga – an intensified stage of *prema*; a stage in the development from *prema* up to *mahābhāva*. In *Ujjvala-nīlamaṇi* (14.146) *anurāga* has been defined as follows: "Although one regularly meets with the beloved and is well acquainted with the beloved, the ever-fresh sentiment of intense attachment causes the beloved to be newly experienced at every moment as if one has never before had any experience of that person. The attachment that inspires such a feeling is known as *anurāga*."

āśrama – the residence of someone practising spiritual life.

ātmā – the soul.

B

bhajana – spiritual practices, especially hearing, chanting and meditating upon the holy names, form, qualities and pastimes of Śrī Kṛṣṇa.

bhakti – the word *bhakti* comes from the root *bhaj*, which means to serve. Therefore the primary meaning of the word *bhakti* is to render service. The performance of activities meant exclusively for the pleasure of Śrī Kṛṣṇa, which are done in a favourable spirit saturated with love, which are devoid of all other desires and which are not covered by the pursuits of fruitive activity (*karma*) or the cultivation of knowledge aimed at merging one's existence into that of the Lord (*jñāna*), is called *bhakti*.
bhāva – (1) spiritual emotions, love or sentiments. (2) the initial stage of perfection in devotion (*bhāva-bhakti*).
Brahman – the impersonal, all-pervading feature of the Lord, which is devoid of attributes and qualities.
brāhmaṇa – the intellectual class amongst the four castes within the Vedic social system.
brahmānanda – the bliss experienced by merging into the Lord's impersonal aspect, Brahman.
brahmāṇḍa – a single, egg-shaped material universe.

C

cakra – the Lord's disc, used as a weapon to subdue demons.
cāmara – a fan made of the hair of a yak's tail, employed especially as part of the paraphernalia offered to the deity.
candana – sandalwood paste.

D

darśana – seeing, meeting, visiting with, beholding.
dāsya-bhāva – one of the five primary relationships with the Lord that is established in the stage of *bhāva* or *prema*; love for or attraction to the Lord that is expressed in the mood of a servant.
dhāma – a holy place of pilgrimage; the abode of Śrī Bhagavān, where He appears and enacts His transcendental pastimes.

G

ghee – clarified butter.

gopas – the cowherd boys who serve Kṛṣṇa in the mood of intimate friends. This may also refer to the elderly *gopas* who serve Kṛṣṇa in the mood of parental affection.

gopīs – the young cowherd maidens of Vraja, headed by Śrīmatī Rādhikā, who serve Śrī Kṛṣṇa in the mood of amorous love. This may also refer to the elderly *gopīs*, headed by Mother Yaśodā, who serve Kṛṣṇa in the mood of parental affection.

gopī-bhāva – the mood of devotion for Śrī Kṛṣṇa possessed by the cowherd women of Vraja.

H

hari-kathā – narrations of the Lord's pastimes and personal nature.

harināma – the holy name of the Lord, especially referring to the *mahā-mantra*.

hlādinī – this refers to the Lord's internal potency (*svarūpa-śakti*) that is predominated by *hlādinī*. *Hlādinī* is the potency that relates to the *ānanda*, or bliss, aspect of the Supreme Lord. Although the Supreme Lord is the embodiment of all pleasure, *hlādinī* is that potency by which He relishes transcendental bliss and causes others to taste bliss.

J

jīva – the eternal, individual living entity, who in the conditioned state of material existence assumes a material body in any of the innumerable species of life.

jñānī – one who pursues the path of *jñāna*, knowledge directed towards impersonal liberation.

K

karmī – one who engages in pious activities, thinking they will lead to material gain in this world or in the heavenly planets after death.

kila-kiñcita – bodily symptoms of ecstasy. They are explained in Śrīla Rūpa Gosvāmī's *Ujjvala-nīlamaṇi* (*Anubhāṇa-prakaraṇa* 39): "Pride, ambition, weeping, smiling, envy, fear and anger are the seven ecstatic loving symptoms manifested by a jubilant shrinking away, and these symptoms are called *kila-kiñcata-bhāvas.*"

kiśorī – an adolescent girl.

kṛṣṇa-kathā – narrations describing Śrī Kṛṣṇa and His activities.

kṣatriya – the second of the four *varṇas* (castes) in the *varṇāśrama* system; an administrator or warrior.

kuñja – a grove or bower; a natural shady retreat, the sides and roof of which are formed mainly by trees and climbing plants.

kuṅkuma – a reddish powder or liquid used by married women to apply to the part in their hair.

L

laḍḍu – an Indian sweet made from chickpea flour.

M

mādana – highly advanced devotional ecstasy that is experienced when meeting with the object of one's worship.

mādhurya-rasa – one of the five primary relationships with Kṛṣṇa established in the stage of *bhāva* and *prema*; love or attachment towards Kṛṣṇa that is expressed in the mood of a lover. This mood is eternally present in the *gopīs* of Vraja.

mahābhāva – the highest stage of divine love.

māna – an intensified stage of *prema*; a stage in the development from *prema* up to *mahābhāva*. It is described in *Ujjvala-nīlamaṇi* (14.96): "When *sneha* reaches exultation, thus causing one to experience the sweetness of the beloved in ever-new varieties, yet externally takes on a crooked feature, it is known as *māna*."

mantra – a spiritual sound vibration that delivers the mind from its material conditioning and illusion when repeated over and over; a Vedic hymn, prayer or chant.

māyā – the Lord's illusory potency, which influences the living entities to accept the false egoism of being independent enjoyers of this material world.

modana – highly advanced devotional ecstasy that is experienced when separated from the object of one's worship.

N

nirguṇa – literally means "devoid of personal attributes". Refers to the impersonal Brahman.

P

praṇāma – an obeisance.

praṇaya – an intensified stage of *prema*; a stage in the development from *prema* up to *mahābhāva*. It is described in *Ujjvala-nīlamaṇi* (14.108): "When *māna* assumes a feature of unrestrained intimacy known as *viśrambha*, learned authorities refer to it as *praṇaya*." The word *viśrambha* used in this verse means "complete confidence devoid of any restraint or formality". This confidence causes one to consider one's life, mind, intelligence, body and possessions to be one in all respects with the life, mind, intelligence and body of the beloved.

prasāda – literally meaning mercy, especially refers to the remnants of food offered to the deity.

prema – divine love.

pūjā – offering of worship.

puṣpāñjali – an offering of flowers from cupped hands to the Lord or his exalted devotee.

R

rāga – (1) a deep attachment that is permeated by spontaneous and intense absorption in the object of one's affection. The primary characteristic of *rāga* is a deep and overpowering thirst for the object of one's affection. (2) an intensified stage of *prema*; a stage in the development from *prema* up to *mahābhāva*. It is described as follows in *Ujjvala-nīlamaṇi* (14.126): "When *praṇaya* reaches exultation, thus causing even extreme misery to be experienced within the heart as happiness, it is known as *rāga*." In his commentary on this verse Jīva Gosvāmī explains that if by accepting some misery there is a chance of meeting with Kṛṣṇa, then that misery becomes a source of great happiness. And where happiness affords one no opportunity to meet with Kṛṣṇa, that happiness becomes the source of great distress. When such a state is experienced, it is known as *rāga*. (3) a classical Indian melody.

rāgānuga-bhakti – an elevated stage of devotion that is motivated by spontaneous attraction or love.

rāgātmikā – one in whose heart there naturally and eternally exists a deep spontaneous desire to love and serve Śrī Kṛṣṇa. This specifically refers to the eternal residents of Vraja.

rākṣasī – a demoness.

rasa – the spiritual transformation of the heart that takes place when the perfected state of love for Kṛṣṇa, known as *rati*, is converted into "liquid" emotions by combination with various types of transcendental ecstasy.

rāsa-līlā – Śrī Kṛṣṇa's dance with the *vraja-gopīs*, which is a pure exchange of spiritual love between Kṛṣṇa and the *gopīs*, His most confidential servitors.

rasika – one who relishes the mellows of devotion (*rasa*) within his heart.

S

sac-cid-ānanda – that which is eternal, composed of spiritual consciousness and full of transcendental bliss.

sādhaka – one who follows a spiritual discipline with the objective of achieving pure devotion for Śrī Kṛṣṇa.

sādhana – the stage of devotional life in which a spiritual discipline is performed for the purpose of bringing about the manifestation of ecstatic, pure love for Śrī Kṛṣṇa (*bhāva*).

sādhu – a saintly person.

sādhya – the goal of one's spiritual practice.

sakhā – a male friend, companion or attendant.

sakhī – a female friend, companion or attendant.

sakhya-bhāva – one of the five primary relationships with Kṛṣṇa that are established in the heart at the stage of *bhāva* or *prema*; love or attachment for the Lord that is expressed in the mood of a friend.

śālagrāma-śilā – self-manifesting deities of Nārāyaṇa in the form of small, round black stones that are found in the Gandakī River in the Himalayas.

sampradāya – a school of religious thought.

saṁvit – this refers to the internal potency (*svarūpa-śakti*) that is predominated by *saṁvit*. It is the potency that relates to *cit*, the cognisant aspect of the Supreme Lord. Although the Supreme Lord is the embodiment of knowledge, *saṁvit* is the potency by which He knows Himself and causes others to know Him.

sannyāsa-daṇḍa – a stick carried by *sannyāsīs*, renunciants in the fourth stage of life according to the Vedic social system.

sarva-śaktimān – the Supreme Lord, Śrī Kṛṣṇa, who possesses all potencies.

śloka – a Sanskrit verse.

sneha – an intensified stage of *prema*; a stage in the development from *prema* up to *mahābhāva*. It is described in *Ujjvala-nīlamaṇi* (14.79): "When *prema* ascends to its ultimate limit, intensifies one's perception of the object of love, and melts the heart, it is known as *sneha*."

sūrya-pūjā – worship of Sūryadeva, the sun-god.

svarūpa-siddhi – the advanced stage of devotional life in which a devotee's *svarūpa*, internal spiritual form and identity, becomes manifest.

T

tapasvī – one who practises austerities as part of his spiritual path.

tulasī – a sacred plant whose leaves and blossoms are used by Vaiṣṇavas in the worship of Śrī Kṛṣṇa; the wood is also used for chanting beads and neck beads.

V

varṇāśrama-dharma – the Vedic social system, which organises society into four occupational divisions (*varṇas*) and four stages of life (*āśramas*).

vastu-siddhi – the stage in which the *vastu*, or the substantive entity known as the *jīva*, is fully liberated from matter. After giving up the material body, the living entity who has already attained *svarūpa-siddhi* enters into Śrī Kṛṣṇa's manifest pastimes, where or he or she receives the association of Kṛṣṇa and His eternal associates for the first time. There one receives further training from His eternal associates. When one becomes established in the mood of their *prema* and one's eternal service to Kṛṣṇa, one gives up all connection with this world and enters His spiritual abode. At this point the *jīva* becomes situated in his pure identity as a *vastu*, and this is known as *vastu-siddhi*.

vātsalya-bhāva – one of the five primary relationships with Kṛṣṇa that are established in the stages of *bhāva* or *prema*; love or attachment for the Lord expressed in the mood of a parent.

vipralambha-bhāva – the loving mood that is felt when separated from one's beloved.

viśuddha-sattva – the state of unalloyed goodness; the quality of existence that is beyond the influence of material nature; Śrīdhara Svāmī has defined *viśuddha-sattva* in his commentary on a verse from the *Viṣṇu Pūrāṇa* (1.2.69): "*tad evaṁ tasyās try-ātmakatve siddhe yena svaprakāśatā-lakṣaṇena tad-vṛtti-viśeṣeṇa svarūpaṁ vā svarūpa-śakti-viśiṣṭaṁ vāvirbhavati, tad-viśuddha-sattvaṁ tac-cānya-nirapekṣas tat-prakāśa iti jñāpaṁ jñāna-vṛttikatvāt saṁvid eva. asya māyayā sparśābhāvāt viśuddhatvam* – the Lord's *cit-śakti* is known as *svaprakāśa*. The term *svaprakāśa* means that it reveals itself and illuminates others also. Just as when the sun rises, it makes itself known and illuminates other objects, so when *cit-śakti* arises in the heart, one can know what is *cit-śakti* and one can know oneself in one's true spiritual identity. Because the *cit-śakti* is *svaprakāśa*, its *vṛtti* is also *svaprakāśa*. The word *vṛtti* literally means function, which refers to the active agency through which the *cit-śakti* operates. The *cit-śakti* is composed of *hlādinī*, *sandhinī* and *saṁvit*. The particular *svaprakāśa-vṛtti* of this threefold *cit-śakti* that reveals Bhagavān, His form and the transformations of His *cit-śakti*, such as His associates and *dhāma*, is known as *viśuddha-sattva*. In other words *viśuddha-sattva* is the self-revealing agency of the *cit-śakti* through which the Lord and His paraphernalia are revealed to the devotees. Because it has no contact whatsoever with the external energy, it is known as *viśuddha-sattva*."

Y

yavana – a barbarian.

yogī – one who practices the *yoga* system with the goal of realisation of the Supersoul or of merging into the Lord's personal body.

yuga – one of the four ages described in the Vedas: Satya-yuga, Tretā-yuga, Dvāpara-yuga and Kali-yuga. The duration of each *yuga* is said to be, respectively: 1,728,000; 1,296,000; 864,000; and 432,000 years. The descending numbers represent a corresponding physical and moral deterioration of mankind in each age.

Verse Index

A

D

E

G

H

I

J

K

M

N

P

R

S

T

V

Y

Worldwide Centers & Contacts

Please contact us at the address stamped or written on the first page of this book, or at the listings below:

INDIA

- **Mathura** - Sri Kesavaji Gaudiya Matha
  Jawahar Hata, U.P. 281001 (Opp. Dist. Hospital)
  Tel: 0565 250-2334, e-mail: mathuramath@gmail.com
- **New Delhi** - Sri Ramana-vihari Gaudiya Matha
  Block B-3, Janakpuri, New Delhi 110058
  (Near musical fountain park) Tel: 011 25533568, 9810192540
- **New Delhi** - Karol Bagh Center - Rohini-nandana
  9A/39 Channa Market, WEA, Karol Bagh
  Tel.: 9810398406, 9810636370, Email: purebhakti.kb@gmail.com
- **Vrindavan** - Sri Rupa-Sanatana Gaudiya Matha
  Dan Gali, U.P. Tel: 0565 244-3270
- **Vrindavan** - Gopinath Bhavan
  Ranapat Ghat, Seva Kunja, Vrindavan 281121, U.P.
  Tel: 0565 244-3359, e-mail: vasantidasi@gmail.com
- **Jagannath Puri** - Jayasri Damodar Gaudiya Math
  Chakratirtha. Tel: 06752-229695
- **Bangalore** - Sri Madana Mohan Gaudiya Matha
  245/1 29th Cross, Kaggadasa pura,Balaji layout, Bangalore-93
  Tel: 08904427754 e-mail: giridharidas@gmail.com

USA

- **Gaudiya Vedanta Publications Offices**
  Tel: (800) 681-3040 ext. 108, e-mail: orders@bhaktiprojects.org
- **Houston** - Preaching Center
  Tel: (1) 713-984 8334, e-mail: byshouston@gmail.com
- **Los Angeles** – Sri Sri Radha Govinda Temple
  305 Rose Avenue, Venice, California 90291
  Tel: (1) 310-310 2817

UNITED KINGDOM & IRELAND

- **Birmingham** - International Distributor
  Tel: (44) 153648-1769, e-mail: jivapavana@googlemail.com
- **London** - Ganga-mata Gaudiya Matha
  Email: gangamatajis@yahoo.co.uk
- **Galway** - Family Center,
  Tel: 353 85-1548200, e-mail: loveisgod108@hotmail.com

GUYANA

- **East Cost Demerara**- Sri Sri Radha Govinda Gaudiya Matha
  156 Area A Bladen Hall School Road
  Tel: 0592 270-4102, 0592 233-2898
  e-mail: radhagovindagy@yahoo.com